I0114530

China's Asia-Pacific Strategy and India

China's Asia-Pacific Strategy and India

Dr Narendra Kumar Tripathi

(Established 1870)

Published in association with
United Service Institution of India
New Delhi

Vij Books India Pvt Ltd
New Delhi (India)

Published by

Vij Books India Pvt Ltd
(Publishers, Distributors & Importers)
2/19, Ansari Road, Darya Ganj
New Delhi - 110002
Phones: 91-11-43596460, 91-11- 65449971
Fax: 91-11-47340674
e-mail : vijbooks@rediffmail.com

ISBN: 978-93-80177-43-4

Contents

Preface

At the outset I must confess that this work on China, has been completed, without any trip to the country. A visit would have been ideal, which would have imparted 'correct' perceptions about Chinese society and life. But by no means its academic worth is reduced, without sounding apologetic for 'misperceptions', one of the fundamental principles of international politics is that perceptions/ misperceptions count. Robert Jervis in his 1976 masterpiece *Perception and Misperception in International Politics* has established this. The views, which have been argued in this book, are as much a product of enduring perceptions of China and its rise and implications for the region. Though, apprehensive that this adds to the burgeoning literature on China, which have been studying its rise. One of the shortcomings in copious literature on China's rise is that, it stresses on the belligerence of China rise. It is understandable, that China still poses much of uncertainty, and its rapid pace of growth in economic, technological, infrastructure and military fields, and makes strategic scenario unpredictable. Chinese rapid progress has taken everybody by surprise. It is important from the Indian perspective that it takes a long-term consistent policy on China. China has made tremendous progress in its regional periphery. Though, in the last two decades India has begun to join in the reorientation of strategic studies focusing on China. This has become the predominant trend in international relations especially in the post-Cold War world. Indian Strategic discourse has kept with the trends of China study, and using their viewpoints to support or counter their analyses. But it can be said that the core of Indian strategic thinking has an apprehension of China, whether articulated or not, but how much it has translated into actual practice is difficult to say. This point can be judged by the fact that though India's military modernisation is rapidly taking place and new bases are being established bordering China, from Ladakh to the northeast, but seeing the continuing long-term desirability of matching China's capabilities and strategic orientation, it will not be wrong to say that India's China focus has been more academic than practical.

If one has to look for the reasons, for India's inadequate securitisation of rise of China, it can be traced in India's larger strategic culture and history. India's self- confining role in South Asia has been behind this, and even this has been arrived at or pushed through various national and international developments, the most prominent being 1962 war. It must be added that India has entered into the global diplomacy with much promise and high profile especially under the leadership of Nehru. It may not be misplaced to say that Nehru's strengths have been India's strength and Nehru's weakness has been India's weakness. In the post-Nehru period India has lost the vision, which was central to Nehru's world view.

This has increasingly become confined due to both leadership as well as international developments. While this may be the historical account of India's regional and global strategy, but in the contemporary times, the circumstances have changed. Now what one is looking at is India sharing space with China in the resurgent Asia. But this term of re-occupying has to be negotiated and cannot be just a product of western analysis of the new geopolitical equations.

Here comes the need to see how China and India relations are to be forged. Are the relations to be seen in just bilateral terms, which have a strong traction. The relations become just a matter of internecine conflict over military build-up, suspicious intentions and border negotiations. Or the problems over Chinese help to Pakistan. The relations have a larger context, the central to which is that how the regional and global system shapes up and how it is to be shaped. If in this context Sino-India rivalry takes place it will in the larger context of regional periphery. Even in this regional rivalry, competing institutionalisation and norms establishment will be seen. In fact, this is already being seen as the countries push for new regional institutions and try to adapt the old ones to the new situation. This book tries to fill this gap where China's Asia-Pacific Strategy is looked at and trend lines are traced on China's strategy and its implications for the region.

It seeks to see how China looks at the medley of relations in the Asia-Pacific. One of the central ideas guiding this research is that it is unhelpful to see China's rise in twin binary dispositions, viz., China as belligerent or China as benevolent. This analysis reflects more on one's aspirations and anxieties. A dispassionate analysis of China is made difficult by hyperbole around it, but it will be wiser to see that it is a country whose nature, characteristics and features are natural for country of its size, and development. In fact, the Chinese ruling elite has often asserted this China is only a developing country. China's natural growing power, will give means at its disposal, which will alter geopolitical configurations of the Asia-Pacific. Even though many mechanisms, which have a long and near permanent presence, will inevitably have to change when China emerges as the predominant power. How this will happen and what are the best mechanisms, which can help in managing China's rise, is the moot point? These are some of the issues, which this book seeks to explore.

In the end it remains for me to thank a lot of people, who have immensely benefited me, in this academic pursuit. This is my first book, therefore it was quite obvious that I had many teething troubles, the interesting part was that while my teeth was growing the pain may have been felt by others. The Director of the institution Lt. Gen. (Retd) P K Singh, encouraged me to go for a book, rather than a monograph. During the working of this monograph, much change in the institutional set–up has taken place. I must thank preceding Director Lt Gen. (Retd) Satish Nambiar, under whose tenure this project started. He has been of inestimable support and inspiration. My tentative steps in China study has been taken with support and encouragement of China expert Brigadier (Retd) Arun Sahgal, previous Head of Research at CS3. One man who was instrumental in helping me finish this project was new Head of Research at CS3 Cmde. Rajeev Sawhney, though a sailor, he has all qualities of infantrymen. His constant pressure on me to finish the project made me finish it earlier otherwise it could have lingered on. Lt Gen (Retd) VK Kapoor was one of the earliest Chairpersons of a presentation, as I took my first steps in a think tank. I am especially indebted to discussants and chairpersons of presentation, who have helped me immensely with their key inputs Col (Retd) PK Gautam, Ambassador (Retd) SK Bhutani, Ambassador (Retd) Ranjit Gupta, Commodore (Retd) Ranjit Rai, Prof. GVC Naidu, Dr Vijay Sakhuja, Dr Abanti Bhattacharya and Commander K K Agnihotri. Thanks are also due to Brig (Retd)Vinod Anand, who has always been available for support. Dr Sudha Raman, former Research Coordinator at USI-CS3, was a key functionary when this project started. Maj Gen (Retd) PJS Sandhu Deputy Director (Editor) and Col (Retd) VK Singh, Deputy Director (Administration) have been a pillar of strength when much institutional change was taking place. I am also thankful to the staff and colleagues erstwhile and present who have made my stay at USI-CS3 pleasant. It's my duty to thank my teachers in JNU who have taught me whatever little I know of academics, in particular Prof Varun Sahni, Prof. Kanti Bajpai, Prof. Sushil Kumar, Prof CSR Murthy, Prof Surjit Mansingh and Prof Amitabh Mattoo. No words can describe contribution of parents and family members for they are the first teachers. Last, but not least I would like to mention a novel *The Good Earth*, by Nobel prize winning author Pearl S. Buck, which could get access in my schooldays it conveyed essential similarity between Indian and Chinese peasant societies.

- Author

Chapter I

Introduction: China's Glance Outside

Introduction

Analysis of China's rise depends upon the theoretical lens applied to study its growth. While a deductive inquiry, may be more theoretically consistent, but its biases will artificially ignore or belittle other substantial events and processes. At the same time, an inductive enquiry is more likely to be a comprehensive approach delineating key events and processes, but may end up as enumerating and filing exercise. A judicious mixture of both these approaches may give a better understanding of China, but the problem is its *sui generis* nature. China defies many classical states characteristics and tendencies, even though its rise has been the most read story in the past decade.[1]

The most prominent characteristic is the economic orthodoxy of liberalisation, free trade and openness. China is one of the rare countries where a strong and powerful communist party rules but is more committed to international trade than its communist principles. In fact, CCP (Chinese Communist Party) derives its popular sustenance from economic growth induced prosperity. The realisation that open economy is the only viable option, came in late 1970s, when the world was still divided between communist empires and free trade liberal zones. It is significant that this realisation came long time before when 'end of history' was achieved in 1989 with the fall of Soviet Empire. China's present economic growth was laid in the year 1978 under the guidance of Deng Xiaoping. This dichotomy produces its own stresses and ironies. Chinese Communist elite have a near consensus on government policies and programs but its overseeing of accompanying institutional capacities is far from the 'open' market principles. While the larger free market enterprise is governed by state controlled capital and industrial enterprises. In this feature the efficacy of the neo-liberal institutional approaches to China's rise is difficult to be trustworthy. One of the cardinal principles of neo-liberal institutional approaches is a multiple channel of international interactions leading to formation of transnational stakeholders, which has an interest in global peace.[2] China from mid-1990s has entered into a number of institutional arrangements.[3] Yet, China has been a free rider to many such arrangements, as in United Nations Security Council, China's role has been an opportunistic fence sitter. In many of the arrangements it has been part of ASEAN derivative ones, it has been more an opportunistic arrangement to take part in regional economic growth. Further, China's rise from grand strategy of not taking pre-mature leadership will militate against the core principles of neo-liberal institutionalism. Therefore China's global diplomacy remains a 'glance outside'. While Chinese attempts to play and shape the regional institutional landscape is important, but its drivers and stakeholders are different.

Its economic growth is stupendous but per capita income is hardly near the developed world. China domestically suffers from economic inequality; its Ginni coefficient is high at 0.473[4]. In order to emerge as the manufacturing hub, it had to compromise on environmental standards, which is beginning to show deleterious effects. Its environmental health is serious enough to merit attention at the highest level. It possesses one of the highest polluted cities of the world. Water pollution has emerged as one of the most baneful effects of uncontrolled industrialisation.[5]

China is basking in the glory of the economic growth, where it has world's highest foreign exchange reserves; in fact it has become the biggest lender of world's biggest economy, United States. It has invested in more than a trillion dollars in the United States treasury bonds. It is unclear that this status of creditor will give it geopolitical advantages, but it is palpable that it is giving good diplomatic coverage.[6] Even in its best foot forward, is not without questions. Its mechanism of accounting and bookkeeping is not at par with global standards. Its composition of Gross Domestic Product (GDP) is questioned, where is argued that State Owned Enterprises (SOE) own a large portion, where accounting and book keeping is not according to the global standards. State intervention in market in China is generally called Beijing Consensus. This has acquired a new respectability after the global economic crisis 2008. Beijing Consensus as against Washington consensus, allows state to 'manage' markets through such mechanisms like, currency stabilisation. Further, they cannot claim of following labour standards, where people have to under go many difficulties without adequate protection from the state over labour standards.

China's political stability though not under question in near term, is also not without pitfalls.[7] Will China manage to ride the growing expectations of its people, as it is now witnessing protests more regularly, especially over environmental problems? A select group of political leaders can hope to manage this rising expectations, or will it lead to unravelling of the political structure. Or rising expectations, economic growth with lack of responsive government will lead to alteration in character of the state.[8] Then the larger questions arise will this unravelling lead to domestic implosion or have international ramifications as well.

The question of Chinese nationalism comes up, will the ruling elite trying to gain legitimacy and control of the state by unleashing nationalism? Or public opinion, which feels stifled on other counts, is likely to be seen as becoming more nationalistic, especially in cyber world. Post-Tiananmen China democracy is likely to be a subject proscribed. As the anxieties of ruling class show in control of cyber world in China. Aggressive nationalism is more likely to lead to international clashes, over territory and resources. Neighbouring countries like India, Japan, Vietnam, Philippines Brunei, Taiwan, etc. will especially come under the receiving side of the development. Though the general belief is that democracy will be an unalloyed benefit to Chinese people, transformation from a communist authoritarian state to democracy, may produce many undesirable effects like, an unbridled nationalism, leading to irredentist claims on neighbouring countries. While the smaller state will have no choice but to give in to an aggressive superpower, but will India, a power in its right, will not like to be seen as capitulating to its bigger neighbour. Especially in a context where it had a border clash with it in 1962. This becomes especially difficult in the contemporary period where Sino-Indian relations are not without its problem over territory. Sino-Indian border extending of 1200 miles, has disputes all over from the northern post in Ladakh to the eastern Arunachal Pradesh. Tibetan problem will always be there even if India does its best to allay the Chinese suspicions.

Chinese growth presents challenges in non-traditional security aspect as well. Migration of people in the far eastern side of Siberian territory of Russia is a recurring problem in Sino-Russian relations. China's expertise in weather modification is likely to be a problem over its contiguous territories. In other aspects like epidemics (SARS, Avian Flu) China's cooperation will be essential.

China has emerged as one of the important parties on the environmental negotiations globally. This could be no more apparent than in Copenhagen Conference on Climate Change. China is one of the highest cumulative emitter of greenhouse gases. In global environmental regime China has to take steps in reducing greenhouse gas. Further, China domestically is also witnessing harmful consequences of unbridled economic growth. The local bureaucracy has conveniently overlooked or connived with industrial enterprises to lead to one of the most polluted surface water systems in China. China has accepted voluntary reduction in emissions. While the global warming and its after effects will be affecting globally and they may result in random local effects. But in case of one aspect China, affects it neighbouring countries vitally that is of transboundary rivers. Many countries which are co-riparian with China on transboundary water courses are facing difficulties over its hydrobehaviour. China has been unilateral in setting up of water projects on the transboundary river water courses. Countries like Russia have complaints over use of water as in the cases of river poisoning in Songhua river.

Despite China becoming one of the most studied countries of the world, it has many contrarian tendencies to offer. This leads to analytic confusion from international relations perspective like China as a 'fragile superpower'.[9] Many statistics are very much of a developing country, which is often asserted by the Chinese leaders. It cannot be denied that present day China gives a kaleidoscopic view of the country. But an 'inside' view of China, its domestic problems, economic inequalities and environmental problems do not give the complete picture. However, pressing they may be for the country's leaders. But cumulative analysis of China, especially from 'outside' gives a completely different picture. It is not being argued that 'inside' and 'outside' are not linked or that they do not form a continuum. But however much globalisation has proceeded, practically no country can claim a conflation of this 'inside' and 'outside'. Especially from strategic studies perspective this analytical juxtaposition should be guarded against. In this hiatus between 'inside' and 'outside', the locus and focus of inquiry is different. In

Waltzian terms 'outside' is anarchic[10], international linkages may be trying to diminish the anarchical aspect of 'outside' by setting up regimes, trades linkages, societal cross flows.[11] But no state has been able to move forward to extend the defining feature of 'inside', viz., obligation and duty to 'outside' which is still governed by charity and real politic convenience. Therefore, internally China how much variegated it may be, externally, it is a regional behemoth with according history to show.

It is here that much China analysis takes a contradictory view of China. It must also be added that many of the contradictions mutually cancel out. In fact, many streams are concurrently present. But a China study also raises the questions of what overarching theoretical lens should one take to ascertain China's future behaviour? While under the theoretical premises of realism and neo-classical realism, China is pursuing its national interest defined as power. Here the concept of national interest is in terms of comprehensive national power. While all states can be seen to doing this, advancing their national power through a comprehensive development of capabilities. This becomes special in the context of China's domestic structure. China is known for its totalitarian and authoritarian structure, while many developments proceed as a matter of increasing the life standards of people, Chinese elite is guided by the aims of increasing Chinese power. That is here an element of competition creeps in especially from the theoretical lens of neo-classical realism. Chinese access for resources is not only means of providing resources but also a means of 'securing' resources in politico-security context. It is notable in the case of China, that in its world view, the traditional theories of international relations like realism and neo-realism, do not adequately account for wars, rather wars are fought for 'scramble of resources'.[12] While many facets of Chinese international behaviour which are very natural to global elite become a part of Chinese power aggrandisement. [13] It is here the theoretical lens become important in sifting the ordinary from the geopolitical. But this analysis is very natural for a country which is ruled by communist elite with a great degree of homogeneity of beliefs and values. Especially in a context what changes is a symbolic gesture very fitting for a new leader, as in Hu Jintaos' slogan of 'harmonius world'. It is also important to realise that the change sought is more a change in diplomatic niceties and procedures than a substantial change. What happens in this analytical vacuity is that "hidden realism" takes prominence. As according to William Tow, "resigning oneself to the permanent condition of ambiguity in the Asian security environment appears to be a tacit concession to the vision of permanent anarchy as inherent to international security relations." [14] That is one is forced to take intentions vs. capabilities debate where capabilities are long term and permanent, but intentions are transitory and fleeting.

A more understated but important issue is Chinese political culture. Chinese political culture known for its bureaucratic hierarchical conception is very secular, especially under the pervading Confucius influence. The influence of Confucian values combined with the bureaucratic conception of society more than politics, makes people passive to the larger governmentality. People are more satisfied in their quotidian lives. Problems emerge only when this daily routine is disrupted or difficult to follow. Environmental protests are especially an apt example. It is recognised by the Chinese government as well, documenting protests on environmental issues, which is growing annually. This is why the Tiananmen incident of 1989, becomes a romantic aberration than a persistent movement. The key to Chinese government accountability will rest on how the proliferating environmental movements are handled by the Chinese elite. Environmental protests contain an explosive amalgamation of peasant protests, corruption of local bureaucracy and bigger problem of sustainability itself. As the rural areas become more integrated in the modern capitalism, it will become increasingly difficult to manage the accompanying problems.

Socially, a new class of Chinese millionaires are coming up who are wards of the CCP functionaries. The mandarins of the Chinese Communist Party are occupying a prominent place in the local hierarchy. Coupled with this is the growing corruption as the new economic growth unleashes money flow in the State Owned Enterprises, in which many party functionary's occupy prominent places. Death penalty has been instituted for the financial corruption, but it is hardly a deterrent.[15] As the institutionalisation of bureaucracy has not taken place, it is increasingly being more manned by the party functionaries. Thus case of accused trying one-self comes up. They are rarely prosecuted. China presents a curious case of an economy whose legal institutions have not kept pace with its economic growth. It is not difficult here to trace the link between 'inside' and 'outside', pressures on domestic stability, along with the imperative to grow economically at competitive prices with other countries on lower industrial scales will have a cascading effect.

Rural peasantry is increasingly coming under stress, economic distribution is not taking place larger systemic exploitation, economic deprivation cooptation of local bureaucracy by the rich urban elite, here the party functionaries are not also leading to safety valve, they are also part of this economic concoction for exploitation. In a peculiar to Chinese social and political practice a new type of leaders have come up, called "burden reduction representatives" or "petitioners representatives".[16] They have over period of time gained expertise in challenging local bureaucracy over rules and regulations and invoke central intervention in their cases. But they are careful enough not to be seen as challenging central governmental authority, but rather local bureaucracy's incompetence and corruption.

Therefore they do not like to call themselves as leaders, but rather burden representatives, who are merely representing an aggrieved local party. Many persons have become a preferred representative over a number of villages.

The rural peasantry though resigned to their fate of being poor cousins to town dwellers, are troubled by the party functionaries conniving with big corporate to produce a rural land grab or resource capture in terms of water flows and water diversions and release of untreated effluents. Here the mitigation mechanism are not in place, or they have atrophied in the new economic melee, party functionaries instead for protecting their rights are more conniving with local bureaucracy and corporate to make a good money. It is here the peasantry's fatalistic attitude is stressed which erupts in public protests and rioting it has forced Chinese central government to abolish agricultural tax in the year 2005.

What are the likely implication of this development while in neo-realist terms these may be unit level characteristic and features will they effect geopolitically? As the peasant restiveness will become "a million mutinies" in a permanent stasis, the state will have to increase its coercive capability to prepare for any contingency. Here the role of military and para-military forces becomes important. China's total number of security officers has increased.[17] People's Liberation Army's role becomes important, as they are the ultimate guarantors of the Chinese Communist Party. This will be the permanent crisis within China, which is more likely to exacerbate than dissipate, and it will defy means of solution as well, it will lead to securitisation of society where paramilitary forces like PAP, PLA become more important. They continue to have relevance in societal affairs and internal politics, this development will have a cascading effect where, it may become permanent feature of the Chinese political culture. Increasing securitisation and militarisation of Chinese polity with self-serving communist elite will have a restive existence. Further, the violence inherent in the Maoist and Communist ideology, will also like to lead to sinister consequences. This internal stasis will have external ramifications as well. Likely to lead to more aggressive foreign policy posture of China.

In the emerging global interdependence China does represent an economic opportunity for its many neighbouring countries, as the contemporary global economic set-up is oriented towards export oriented growth especially western countries, but in future economic growth will have to look at domestic consumption in which the Asian economies have to catch up. As a country which for the last thirty years have focussed to 'outside' for its economic growth. This aspect has generated such anodyne phrases from the elite like "peaceful rise', "peaceful development" and "harmonious world", will increasingly begun to lose their tactical value.[18] China will be impelled to take more aggressive policies at 'outside'. Especially with China having invested so much in cross country infrastructure cannot afford to lead it remain idle, extending from oil fields to pipelines, to ports and road network and above all SLOCs. Especially in the context when outlook shifts from trade to resources. Chinese investment in trans-country infrastructure assets, will aim to engender regional dependency. Presently, they occupy the totemic image of China's regional integration and open economic policy. But will they occupy the same totemic position is difficult to say as regional economic architecture begins to change? In the Southeast Asia region, while China has suffered trade deficits with neighbouring countries, it is not definite that China will not push advantages with the smaller countries. In fact, when big countries are beginning to realign their positions, smaller countries will have no choice but to follow.

China's Geopolitical Dilemmas

Asian geopolitics grapples with the rise of China. China has managed to position itself as the main contender of United States regional influence. China positing itself in dyadic terms with United States, is a manifestation of the Chinese desire to reclaim its great power status. It is also desired from the fact that China's prime security interest is Taiwan, and whose sole guarantor is the United States. Therefore, an element of competition is inevitable in the relationship of the two countries. Yet, is also noteworthy how China has managed to ascend its position in the region. Chinese worldview sees the region as Sinocentric that is China occupying central place, with the countries surrounding it owing a special obligation to the country. This is generally referred to as China's Middle Kingdom complex.

China has suffered from historical difficulties like Great Leap Forward and Cultural Revolution. These were brutal movements involving a heavy loss of men and material. In this background Deng Xiaoping formulated policies, which continue to guide nations foreign policy. China began to focus on economic modernisation and opening up of the country. Deng Xiaoping ushered in reforms, which were less brutal and xenophobic. Present day China in large part owes to the strategic policies formulated and practiced by Deng Xiaoping. He formulated a policy of 24 characters, which emphasised on biding time and waiting opportune moment for taking leadership.

This policy not only entailed that China has managed to follow an incremental policy of modernisation but also stabilisation. Hence China has been careful in forging and managing relations. The realisation has dawned that China will have to take help of outside powers in the rapid progress of country. From the 1980s, China has managed to open up its economy, and international relations. From 1980s and to 2007, China has managed to quadruple its GDP. The manner of Chinese economic growth is equally important. China has become workshop to the world. This is especially important, for China has managed to develop synergies with neighbouring countries, in engendering a mutual economic beneficial relationship. China has become regions economic locomotive. This is especially important as compared with India, which has seen economic growth in services sector, but has not managed to share the economic growth the neighbouring countries. Hence the synergies are absent, thus India continues to be on its solitary path of economic growth. But in case of China, the threat is that China in its rising economic interdependence will at its time of choosing began to exercise political power.

China's Regional Periphery

China's rise has created geopolitical ripples which has forced many countries to align their policies with its new found status and influence. It cannot also be denied that the China's rise is an unparallel event in the history of international relations. It is the most analysed rise of a country. China has been equally careful, not to ruffle feathers on its rise. Chinese obsession with secrecy and control has managed to control much of the negative repercussions of the rise. Chinese are conscious of the geopolitical implications of the rise, and the likelihood of conflict which it may generate between the status-quoist powers and the revisionist powers. In case of China this fear is all the more palpable for the country is surrounded by fourteen land neighbours, most of which it did not have good relations with. In the period of Cold war, ideological brotherhood could not prevent a Sino-Soviet split in 1969, which was accompanied by the bloody clashes along the Ussuri River. Sino-Japan relations are still rattled by the historical baggage of Japanese colonialism. Japanese Prime Ministers visit to the Yasukuni shrine; US-Japanese Defense partnership under which nearly fifty thousand

US troops are stationed in Japan. The US- Japanese defence partnership is though of the Cold War era, but it is one of the defining security features of the region, as repeatedly emphasised by the United States. Even though recently, strains have come in over the re-location of Okinawa base, yet it cannot be denied that partnership remains strong as ever.

Japan independently of the United States is a competitor for regional influence. It possesses one of biggest economies of the world. Though, its defense expenditure is minimal as compared to the percentage of the GDP. Yet, it cannot be denied that it possesses one of the most technologically able industrial base, which can multiply its military power. Japanese are content with the existing security arrangement which, predominantly relies on the United States nuclear umbrella. Japan has restricted its posture to be defensive. China and Japan have dispute over territory as well over Senkaku islands as in East China Sea. From the Chinese perspective, it is important that Japan does not 'normalise' and practise policies independent of United States. While Japan is taking cognizance of the growth in power and position of PRC, and seeing the regional states including United States beginning to accommodate China. It has to somehow make diplomatic recognition of the new position of China. How it does this, with defense partnership continuing to be fulcrum of its defense, will be interesting to watch. With already as worlds number three economy, and poised to become number two in the years to come. In the long term Japan will have to realign its regional diplomacy.

India comes lower on priority in its external glance. China is aware of the potential and adequateness of Pakistan to hem in India in the sub-regional focus of South Asia. Further, India still occupies a marginal presence to the regional geopolitical focus of Asia-pacific or East Asia. The contours of the region are still under contest, and

India claim for a rightful presence in the larger Asia Pacific is not beyond debate. China has been trying to prevent India from expanding its regional presence to wider Asia-pacific. Though, China is generally dismissive of Indian claims to great power status, and accuses it of regional hegemonism. But it has begun to take note of India, especially in the wake of Indo-US nuclear deal. It symbolised the growing importance of India in the regional geopolitical calculus, where United States led in making one time exception for India in it non-proliferations rules. Of all the countries which are territorially contiguous to China, Sino-India border is the most troubled one, which has also lead to border conflict in 1962. Along the border there is much of action taking place, especially on the side of the Indian border. India is military fortifying its presence. But it cannot be said that China is taking note of the activities on the border. Rather, it gives a sanguine disregard to the military threat posed by India. China is confident of its military superiority. Yet it is also unlikely that growing Indo-US relations and growing Indian military might may have gone un-noticed from Chinese military strategist's point of view.

Another neighbour of China, South Korea is also part of the traditional 'hub and spoke' alliance of the United States. China cannot ignore that South Korea, with which it has recently started its relations is host to around thirty thousand troops (28,500). Its traditional ally North Korea is suffering from dangers of implosion, with extreme autarchic policy, while continues to pose a challenge to the regional security by its nuclear explosion and missile testing. China is actively cooperating with other countries under Six Party Talks to solve the North Korean nuclear proliferation issue.

United States strong influence in the South East Asian countries like Thailand, Singapore and Philippines cannot be discounted either. Singapore has strong relations with the United States. Thailand follows policy of equidistant friendly relations with countries. Philippines at one time had the world's second largest military base outside United States, which United States has withdrawn. Despite the growing economic and political influence of China in the East Asia and South East Asia, China cannot be oblivious of the military content of the United States presence in its regional periphery. Whatever, doubts were over South East Asia low in priority in United States foreign policy, it has countered it by signing Treaty of Amity and Cooperation with ASEAN and US-ASEAN Summit, which has been on the table since 2003. To add to its regional commitment it has also appointed an Ambassador for ASEAN. And the most obvious of all United States has strong military presence in the region independent of all other countries. Pacific Forces Command with headquarters at Hawaii is capable of influencing regional neighbourhood.

PRC's one China policy and integration of Taiwan into mainland is plagued by United States support for the later. While US supports peaceful and democratic integration, China has not renounced use of force in relations to Taiwan, declaring independence. China has used its growing geopolitical clout to make states restrict their engagement with Taiwan. Taiwan has been getting arms from United States, which Beijing routinely objects.

Despite the clamour of China's rise, it will also not go beyond Chinese comprehension that it is heavily surrounded by United States military footprint, which extends right from Japan in Northeast Asia to Afghanistan in South Asia. With gradual decline in Pakistan's strategic depth in Afghanistan, China will be especially apprehensive of the growing Indo-US convergence. While the regional and global security discourse does not talk in containment terms, yet it cannot be overlooked that many alliances are the relic of the same period. China's glance outside is bound to be a continuum of its policy during the Cold War. Though it was on the side of the victors, it was only a consolation. It has to see that its economic and political development do not raise the hackles of the powers be. It is not that China has been cowed into submission by the US military footprint in its periphery. In 1950 it forced US to stop along the 38th parallel. It also indulged in military clash with India in 1962 and with Vietnam in 1979.

China began to gradually open up its economy to technological growth and modernisation. This has put China in the front line of the states today. In this quest for economic growth and modernisation, a stable periphery was the most important requirement. This explains China's modest behaviour internationally. Yet it was not without occasional sparring as evident in the Chinese clashes in the South China Sea over the Spratlay's island. In the recent times the Chinese have behaved aggressively by undertaking anti-Satellite test (A-SAT) in the year 2007, aggressive patrolling on Sino-Indian borders. It is one of the important developments, which give rise to the fears of militarization of space. China has also been involved in a naval sparring incident with the United States ship *Impeccable* in the South China Sea.

It cannot mask the Chinese cautious approach in forging its diplomatic relations in the external arena. China has been cautious not to involve itself in any incident which results in incurring any burden internationally. Chinese grand strategy proscribed any undertaking of pre-mature burden. As they perceived that China is still a developing country which cannot afford taking active interest in the international affairs. Further, China was also guided by its self-image of a victim in the international affairs, and saw many international mechanisms as an extension of Western contrivances and means of domination. Thus it was content with glancing outside the regional periphery and sitting at sidelines. This also explains its particular apprehension of multilateral forums. Even though China possessed one of the coveted positions of Permanent Membership in the Security Council with the United Nations. Yet it only sparingly involved itself in major issues of the contemporary international affairs. But was careful enough to use veto sparingly, only in case of its close allies like Myanmar. Chinese apprehension of multilateral diplomacy still is guided by the overall grand strategy of desisting from active involvement in international affairs. Though, this grand strategy is generally argued to change, and it has begun taking interests in regional periphery.

Yet, this policy of forsaking multilateral involvement was increasingly coming into clash with Chinese fundamental interests of keeping its regional and global surrounding peaceful in metaphorical terms. It was in mid-1990s that China began to revise its policy over the multilateral diplomacy, as China was increasingly being identified in a series of writings emerging from the United States, as likely an object of containment. China had no option but to pre-empt this coalescing of opinion and forces threatening to engulf it. The realisation was dawning that, if China has to keep its regional periphery stable and peaceful, an autarchic policy will not be sufficient. But it will have to act at least regionally, in order to clear the apprehensions of its neighbours. Friendly neighbours are the best ambassadors of Chinese good intentions.

While sitting on sidelines is a good strategy at the Security Council, it may be self defeating in the regional stage. Especially in a surrounding which has one of the world's successful regional organisations ASEAN? Curiously it's ironic, that Chinese strategy of regional involvement is guided by the overall logic of minimal involvement in regional affairs of state. Its preference for bilateral dialogue has to give way in the wake of ASEAN's insistence on multilateralism. China also realised that it will have to act multilaterally especially in the wake of its desiraibalility of gaining entry to World Trade Organisation (2001). China had to really work hard to gain entry into the WTO. Its relations with US were critical in this.

Table 1.1

China's Foreign Trade with Asian Countries (in US $ Dollars) in April 2010

Figure in 100 Million USD

Amount / Countr-ies	Total	Increa-se as of 2009 %	Export	Increa-se %	Import	Increa-se %	Balanc-e of Trade 2010	2009
Northe-ast Asia	432.30	39.4	158.73	30.1	273.57	45.5	16.81	131.35
Japan	250.58	35.8	97.79 %	24.6	152.79	44.1	-114.84	-65.93
ROK	176.52	45	58.44	40.9	118.09	47.2	-59.65	-38.78
DPRK	2.3332	18.3	1.6676	27.7	0.6657	-0.2	1.00	0.64
Mongo-lia	2.8687	52.2	0.8412	1.4	2.0275	92.1	-1.19	0.23
Southe-ast Asia/ ASEAN	241.95	52.0	113.91	42.6	128.04	61.5	-14.13	0.56
Brunei	1.5373	771.0	0.387	76.5	1.2286	75274.-8	-0.92	0.17
Burma	3.3798	63.8	2.5602	57.0	0.8196	89.4	1.74	1.20
Cambo-dia	1.3379	49.1	1.2851	46.8	0.0528	143.6	1.23	0.85

contd/-

Amount / Countr-ies	Total	Increa-se as of 2009 %	Export	Increa-se %	Import	Increa-se %	Balanc-e of Trade 2010	2009
Indone-sia	35.82	66.4	18.07	62.04	17.75	70.6	0.32	0.72
Laos	1.6626	215.2	0.5672	37.4	1.0855	873.5	-0.52	0.30
Malay-sia	61.70	54.8	20.32	20.6	41.38	79.9	-21.06	-6.15
Philipp-ines	22.88	44.8	9.76	44.8	13.12	44.7	-3.36	-2.32
Singap-ore	47.30	36.0	28.27	32.5	19.03	41.7	9.24	7.90
Thaila-nd	42.63	50.2	14.48	56.3	28.16	47.2	-13.68	-9.87
Vietna-m	23.71	56.5	18.29	59.7	5.42	46.8	12.87	7.76
East Timor	0.0308	299.9	0.0308	300.4	-	-100.0	0.03	0.01
South & West Asia	106.51	42.2	63.79	30.2	42.72	64.9	21.08	23.10
India	54.77	46.4	31.59	32.1	23.19	71.7	8.40	10.40
Pakist-an	7.3659	33.9	6.0435	32.9	1.3224	38.7	4.72	3.59
Sri Lanka	1.3783	0.6	1.2954	-1.0	0.0829	35.6	1.21	1.25
Nepal	0.5151	39.5	0.5035	38.7	0.0116	85.4	0.49	0.357
Maldiv-es	0.0439	60.6	0.0438	60.04	0.0001	-100.0	0.044	0.027
Bhutan	0.0004	-57.3	0.0004	-57.3	-	-	0.0004	0.001

China's Asia-Pacific Strategy

China's central strategy on regional periphery is to exercise soft power. This attractive pull is at all spectrum levels. Soft power where sufficient and hard power where necessary. In fact it will be naive to assume that neighbouring states will not acquiesce in the larger shadow of the regional hegemony. Gravitational pull is very strategy for Chinese, that they realise from the example of Soviet Union that challenging the reigning power may bring doom its great power ambitions. Further the context of great power rivalry has changed, US has been able to defeat Soviet Union because of its superior economic might. If China has to do this it will have to replicate United States free capitalism, In fact, Deng's "cat theory" explained this arguing that cat's colour is immaterial as long as it continues to catch mice. Any realist understanding of international relations will predict that rise of any great power is bound to lead to recognition by the smaller powers and consequently accommodation of interests.

Chinese regional diplomacy is exercised by both acting as an economic magnet for the region as well as producing necessary hard power to make states align their power with Chinese interests. In fact, China has been quite successful in this, its policy has been successful both at the regional level where it is said to be the driving force of regional economic growth but also at the global level. China has more aggressively pursued good relations with the United States than perhaps any other country. Its diplomacy of identifying sympathetic friends has been quite helpful in this.[19] China favours engagement from United States, even at the same time maintaining that hegemonistic policies should be opposed. While Chinese strategic culture has a remarkable understanding of discourse politics, which China exercises to the hilt. In this aspect, Sino-US relations are the perfect example. While at the global level China's Defence White Paper argue that there are hegemonistic policies in international relations at work which should be opposed. Further, it favours a multipolar world. It's positioning itself against United States as the alternate pole is fortified by its support for rogue states like North Korea, Myanmar and Iran. In this it is ably helped by its veto power in the United Nations Security Council. But in history of international relations China has waged one of the most patient struggles to forge good bilateral relations with United States.

In the regional periphery it has tried its best to portray a charming face. Its preference for bilateral relations with neighbouring countries of Southeast Asia, has over the period of time more focussed on ASEAN. It has very ably used the ASEAN and its derivative institutions to prevent balancing of forces. While the many ASEAN countries were more interested in socialising China multilaterally, China realised that if it doesn't gets actively involved in the neighbourhood, its strategic interest will be compromised. As in the post-Cold War world many shrill voices of China containment were coming from the United States, Chinese failure to act in mid-1990s to multilaterally engage might have lead to balancing collations against it. Especially in a neighbourhood where under San Francisco alliance system many close US allies were existing. Through the twin means of Chinese militarily engagement and its economic pull, it has been able to dissipate a counter balancing coalition forces against it.

Many regional economic instrumentalities established by China have become a mainstay of economic growth of the neighbouring countries like Vietnam and Laos under Greater Mekong Sub-region (GMS). China also exercised influence in the regional neighbourhood, when it desisted from devaluing its currency in the wake of Asian Financial Crisis. In contemporary times financial means of exercisising this attractive power has increased manifold. Especially in the wake of ongoing global economic meltdown. It has offered much financial mechanism like liberal loans under Chiang Mai

Initiative. Most importantly its investment in US treasury receipts is a prime example of its economic stakes in the global financial system.

However, it is not that China is exercising pull, by conscientiously erasing its hard power from strategic calculus. It is here the Chinese strategic culture of Sun Tzu comes into practice, which enjoins that "waging war is not supreme excellence but in breaking enemy's resistance without fighting" is supreme excellence. Chinese practice has been to increase the policy dilemmas of the countries which are close to United States.[20] There are different viewpoint on this, many analysts maintain that it is not evident neighbouring countries have come to alter their policies with respect to China. There are other analysts who give instance of countries aligning their foreign policy choices with Chinese view in mind. It will be naive to assume that neighbouring countries will not take Chinese interest into account in formulating their policies for the region. As that will be against principles of international relations. Territorially contiguous territories of South East Asia have begun to defer to Chinese interests.

As far as hard power is concerned China is modernising its Peoples Liberation Army. Official Chinese claims on defence budget are doubted and argued that in reality it is higher. China's aim is to be first class military force in the region by 2020. China has categorically said that it will oppose secessionist tendencies in Taiwan and is willing to use force to prevent this. This doctrine of refusing to abjure non peaceful means as given in Article 8, is very well display of the Chinese intentions on use of force. Further, China has taken a number of actions which raise doubts over Chinese intentions, like in Hainan incident, anti-satellite test and some of the very bellicose statements of Chinese generals over the possibility of armed conflagration over Taiwan.[21] In Asia-Pacific Chinese aim for military modernisation, has an in built accounting of asymmetric capabilities, while it will not enter into a direct fight with United

States, and appear to be as conciliatory as possible. But it is likely to use its asymmetric power to its geopolitical advantages in the regional context.

The Chapter on China's Strategic Outlook analyses the Chinese strategic culture which gives its policy a unique advantage over its external relations. Chinese strategic culture combines aggression-defensiveness of a victim, which entails contradictory tendencies at the same time. As in the principles of "active defence", this may legitimise defensive wars. It is followed by Chinese Strategy in North East Asia. Though the endeavour is to look at Chinese policy at Asia-Pacific level, dividing it in sub-regional focuses will serve better analytical purpose. The subsequent chapter focuses on the Chinese strategy in Southeast Asia, where it is argued that it is advantage China. In the next chapter, Indian policy towards Asia-Pacific is discussed and traces the pressures on India to look outside its sub-regional focus of South Asia, and inducements on offer in Asia-Pacific.

A Note on Research Methodology

Before attempting such an ambitious endeavour like gleaning China's Asia-Pacific Strategy, one must clarify the research methods, not least for the reader, but for organising one own analysis and thought patterns. The most important question come up on the subject matter, why China's Asia-Pacific Strategy not China's global strategy? And what is their inter-relation. Has China not embarked on aggressive African diplomacy or Latin American Strategy? First, is China own distinctive formulation. In China National Defence White Paper 2008, the region mentioned is Asia-Pacific. Its reference comes about four times. In the first formulation, it reads as "the Asia-Pacific Security situation is stable on the whole."[22] This formulation comes right at the beginning of the Defence White Paper, just after discussion on global situation. The other references on Asia-Pacific are;

However, there still exist many factors of uncertainty in Asia Pacific security. (p.5)

At the same time, the U.S. has increased its strategic attention to and input in the Asia Pacific region, further consolidating its military alliances, adjusting its military deployment and enhancing its military capabilities. (p.5)

At the 14th ARF Ministerial Meeting in August 2007 China stressed that the new security concept is based on the diversity and common interests of the Asia Pacific region, and accords with the inherent law and requirements of the region's pursuit of peace, development, progress and prosperity. (p. 48)

Though, in the first reference to Asia-Pacific is followed by discussion on SCO (Shanghai Cooperation Organisation), it cannot be denied that China's Central Asia relations are critical to the security of the Xinjiang province as well as major provider of energy requirements. China's spawning of SCO is a manifestation of this belief. At the present moment it will suffice to say that China's interest in Central Asia and South Asia are distinct as compared to what is called generally called East Asia. In our conception of Asia-Pacific, the region's geographical expanse is taken from the western borders of China and India to the headquarters of United States Pacific Command, stationed in Hawaii. This region is not only a geographical construct but also political or geopolitical. That is these states are increasingly seeing heightened strategic activity, which can only be studied and understood in relation to one another.

Secondly, China's Asia–Pacific strategy is focussed also because, of their military capabilities, despite the rhetorical flourish, it is essentially a regional power, with limited means of power projection. It is often cited that China lacks an aircraft carrier, to project its influence. That is, China is predominantly continental power, with limited means of power projection. Though, its ships have participated in anti-piracy operations in Somalia. It intends to increase its naval power projection to Indian Ocean, but its naval capability still remains largely constrained to its periphery.

Thirdly, the argument is from the traditional sphere of influence, great powers like to have a sphere of influence in which they are untrammelled and free from outside interference, howsoever ideal it may be in postulation and compromised in reality. North and South America for United States as asserted in Monroe doctrine; Present day Russia's assertion of special privileges in respect of countries of former Soviet Union. India's desired sphere of influence in South Asia, similarly, Asia-Pacific for China. One of the primary determinants of sphere of influence is dominant power, but if it is coupled with cultural similarities, the claims become more prominent and legitimate. China's cultural history of Sino-centrism, which reflects in quest for East Asia Community, makes it a logical case for sphere of influence. Though variations exist in Chinese cultural influence, but their having similarity cannot be outrightly rejected. Further, ties may be of tributary to patron or just a convenient transactional relationship one could not deny the linkage. Analysts and writers from both the sides have asserted this. More importantly, China's strategy has been to wait for the right time, once China's rise takes place cultural similarity will become important determinant for carving out a regional sphere of influence.

The preceding paragraph was delineating reasons for choosing subject, but more importantly is the methodological tool. Buzan's Regional Security Complex is very popular tool for analysing regional security issues. Regional Security Complex, is ' a set of units whose major processes of securitisation, desecuritisation, or both are so interlinked that their security problems cannot reasonably be analysed or resolved apart one another.'[23] Without going into much detail and advocating RSCs, it will suffice to say that it presents an appropriate framework to study regional security affairs. As states security and insecurity are relational aspects. On the side-lines, it also needs to be asserted such superlative enquiries or research as "all or nothing" especially in case of China is nothing but analytically confusing. China's rise has unleashed a strong regional dynamic, where one cannot study regional security relations without taking into account regional patterns of relations.

(Endnotes)

[1] "China's rise decades most read story" available at http://www.reuters.com/article/idUSTRE5B70AA20091208.

[2] Robert O Keohane, *After Hegemony: Cooperation and Discord in World Political Economy* (Princeton: Princeton University Press, 1984).

[3] Samuel Kim, "China and Uni ted Nations", in El izabeth Econom y and Michel Oskenberg, eds.,*China Joins the W orld: Pr ogress and Pr ospects* (New Y ork: CFR, 1999).

[4] From 1978 to 1984, the Gini Coefficinet in China was at 0.16, while form 1984 the index began to cl imb r eached 0.473 in 2007 . Available at ht tp://business.globaltimes.cn/comment/2010-01/497236.html.

[5] Elizabeth Economy, *The River Runs Black: Environmental Challenge to China's Future* (New Y ork; CFR, 2004).

[6] Daniel W. Drezner, "Bad Debts; Assessing China's Financial Influence in Great Power Politics", International Security, Vol. 34, No. 1, Fall 2009. Author argues

that though his findings ar e preliminary, but ther e ar e "constraints on China' s ability to con vert its financial holdings into pol icy lev erage.", p. 44.

[7] Willy Lam, "China's Political Feet of Clay", *Far Eastern Economic Review,* October 2009, Vol. 172, No .8.

[8] Brantly Womack, "China B etween R egion and W orld", *The China Journal,* No.61, January 2009.

[9] Susan L. Shirk, *China: The Fr agile Superpower* (New York: Oxford University Press, 2007)

[10] Kenneth N. Waltz, *Theory of International Politics* (Reading: Addison Wesley, 1979).

[11] Hedley B ull, *Anarchical S ociety: Study of Or der in W orld Politics* (New Y ork, Sussex: Columbia University Press, 1995).

[12] Michael Pi llsbury, *China: Debates the Futur e S ecurity En vironment,* (Washington,National Defence University Press, 2000), p.xxxii.

[13] Sharon La Franierere , "China Helps the Powerful in Namibia", in *International Herald Tribune,* N ovember 20, 2009, http://www .nytimes.com/2009/11/20/ world/asia/20namibia.html?ref=asia&pagewanted=print.

[14] William T. Tow eds., *Security in the Asia-P acific: A R egional- Global Nexus?* (Cambridge; Cambridge University Press, 2009), p.10.

[15] Andr ew W edeman, 'The I ntensification of Corruption in China" , *The China Quarterly,* No.180, December 2004 .

[16] Lianjiang Li and K evin J. O'B rien, "Pr otest Leadership in China" , *The China Quarterly,* March 2008, No . 193, p .15.

[17] The number of security forces has increased from 658,000 in 1982 to 870,000 in 1995 to 1.4 million by 2006. In addition to the increase in numbers, there is lack of professionalization at lower levels. The data ci ted in Murray Scot Tanner

and Eric Green, " Principals and Secret Agents: Central versus Local Control Over Policing and Obstacles to "Rule of Law" in China", *The China Quarterly*, 191, September 191, September, 2007. See note 59, p. 664.

[18] Daniel Lynch, " Chinese Thinking on the Future of International Relations: Realism as the *Ti,* Rationailsm as the *Yong*? *The China Quarterly* ,197, March 2009, p.88.

[19] Richard H. Solomon, *Chinese Negotiating Behaviour: Pursuing Interests Through 'Old Friends'* (Washington: USIP, 1999).

[20] Evan S Medeiros, *Pacific Currents: The Responses Of US Allies And Security Partners In East Asia To China's Rise* (Santa Monica, CA, Rand, 2008).

[21] Andrew Scobell, "Is there a civil-miltary gap in China's peaceful rise?", *Parameter* Vol. XXXIX, No .2, Summer 2009.

[22] *China's National Defense in 2008*, Information Office of the State Council of the People's Republic of China January 2009, Beijing, available in pdf format at http://www.fas.org/programs/ssp/nukes/2008DefenseWhitePaper_Jan2009.pdf., p.5.

[23] Barry Buzan and Ole Weaver, *Regions and Powers: The Structure of International Security* (Cambridge: Cambridge University Press, 2003), p.44.

Chapter 2

China's Strategic Outlook

Introduction

Strategic Culture stands for a "distinctive and lasting set of beliefs, values and habits regarding the threat and use of force, which have their roots in such fundamental influences as geopolitical setting, history and political culture."[1] As against the rational view of state action and behaviour, strategic culture aims to take a nuanced analysis of inter-state relations. This is in line with the developments in international relation theory, where the earlier dominant approaches of structural realism, which focussed on rational behaviour of states, are giving way to more culturally nuanced analysis of international relations as emphasised in constructivist approaches. Therefore, return of culture and identity is being emphasised.[2] Culturally nuanced analysis is seen as providing enriched explanation to states strategic behaviour, more importantly to the community feeling of states or lack of it. With the help of strategic culture key motivations, preferences of the states can be deciphered. Rather, than following the rational approach to problems in international relations. However, it is also worth noting that with the relative peace in international relations there is more tendency to look for culturing international relations.

Recourse to strategic culture can be taken to know the crisis behaviour of the states. That is, the states are free not only to espouse their cultural preferences in peace time. But also to look for the policy preferences or strategic behaviour state is likely to follow. This may be especially desired in the case of the country like China, which is slated to become a superpower. The black box of foreign policy in case of China is too complicated to give a coherent picture of their perspective on international relations. A delineation of Chinese strategic culture is likely to give us a better picture on Chinese motivations and drivers in foreign policy making.

One can question the efficacy of studying Chinese strategic culture, especially, when international relations are said to be in a post-strategic era.[3] It is difficult to ascribe strong elements of strategic culture of any nation, without having a belief in importance of strategy. Strategy in its classic definition means use of force or threat of force. On the surface, it may look at fairly restricted and limited phenomena especially in the time where there is absence of major wars. But taking this at the face value will give incomplete picture. Firstly, because by its very nature force and threat of force which are the domains of the state, are most powerful force on earth which cannot be supplanted, but only by more force. Therefore, even in its limited utility in an era of peace, at the supra level must assert its importance. Any study of international relations which tends to ignore or downplay this phenomenon will be a mistaken view. Despite the peaceful era in the international relations, the defence spending of nation-states have not reduced. Further, even in the absence of use of force there is no absence of threat of use of force, even if explicitly made or not. In fact, it is not the Woodrow Wilson who decides your strategy it is Hitler which forces your strategy.[4] Strategy as force and threat of force continues to remain as valid as ever, as Gray emphasises that strategy is eternal.[5] But the instruments of strategy are not eternal they have their existence in particular time frame. It is this changed context that a study of strategy and strategic culture is important.

One factor which has changed the strategic landscape in Asia especially and world generally is China's rise. Along with India's rise, present century is termed as Asian Century. While this phrase attests to the new found significance of the Asian country's international affairs. But simultaneously an attempt is made to argue that Asian dominated international relations will be different in comparison to US dominated international order. The claims for difference are difficult to delineate but a large portion of the claims lie in the difference of culture. While the West can be accused of favouring unilateral approach, with prime importance to military force. In comparison, Asian century advocates point to the more inclusivist culture of Asian countries. While the benignness of India is less doubtful at the international stage, it is also because of India being in a less dominating position, but China poses uncertainty of intentions and motives. This may be derived from the fact that presently China is the most likely challenger to the United States and coupled with this is Chinese history and strategic culture attests to its offensive culture.

But as any repeated activity tends to do it familiarises us with the dangerous and lets us to take more sanguinary view of the development. In last one decade regularly positive views on China have been coming out. Even as Chinese stand on many views have not changed like Taiwan, territorial disputes in South China Sea and East China Sea and rapid pace of its military modernisation. Neighbouring states of China continue to be apprehensive of its future role. Thus, in order to arrive at a more comprehensive view of China, it is important to know Chinese strategic culture as working on shared assumptions which are key to nation-state future growth and objectives. Simultaneously, one can see a number of Chinese goals and objectives which are convenient cover to the realpolitique aims and tendencies. It is here that Chinese strategic culture will help in assessing deeply held views.

The problem in any such study is that where to look for the elements of strategic culture, it is obviously simple to look at in the history of cultural practices and policy pronouncements. It cannot be ignored that any society has many strategic cultures existing at the same time that is there is a competing view of strategic cultures. One should guard against cultural reification. But this methodology will give an array of opinions like Johnston's' parabellum culture offensive realists, agreed by Andrew Scobell or a more benign assertion by Huiyun Feng (defensive Confucian realists) and Tiejun Zhang (cultural moralists). Swiane and Tellis assert China is looking for the asymmetric gains. But ascription of strategic culture on past practices, fails to account for changes, both internally and externally.

In strategic studies the bias for high politics, is well entrenched. Sinologists have taken strategic culture to be a near permanent feature of the influences constraining or enabling policies of decision makers in China. But the dynamic of relationship between state and society has to be focussed as well. Characteristics of political culture affecting states international behaviour is often asserted, but a dynamic conception of state-society relation is required. In case of China this dynamic presents one of the key uncertainties in Chinese future. State in society approach has generally been overlooked to understanding and explaining Chinese foreign policy making.

Chinese Strategic Culture/ Outlook

As already discussed strategic culture looks for use or threat of force, but here a wider canvass is attempted, which will influence China's strategic outlook. These ideas may either lead to military modernisation as in the case of Chinese military thought or lead to forging of economic links as in the case of regional economic integration. Chinese strategic outlook can be studied in three broad areas, (i) ideational principles (ii) military thought and (iii) state/ society pressures.

(i) Ideational: Philosophical and Normative Principles

This can be studied in two broad categories one traditional, ideas which have their genesis into Chinese ancient history, second comparatively modern but powerful, though they may look misnomer in the contemporary market economy, is the Marxist, Leninist-Maoist thought. At the ideational level, keys to Chinese thinking patterns can be gleaned from the Confucius thought. Though Confucianism has an uneven history but, it is the most important strand of thought on Chinese behaviour and perspective. As asserted by authors Barry, Chan and Watson, that "if we were to characterise in one word the Chinese way of life for the last two thousand years, the word would be "Confucian".[6] Even more importantly the expanse of the beliefs was irrespective of the trials and tribulations of history. As Barry, Chan and Watson argue that "many Chinese have professed themselves to be Taoists, Buddhists, even Christians, but seldom have they ceased at the same time to be Confucianists."[7] That is, the belief became so popular and people friendly that it became the substratum of other beliefs. Confucianism can be especially attributed for making people shift their gaze from superstitious issues to ordinary lives. It has lead to one of the architects of the societies.

In this aspect it was so successful that it became identified with primitive hierarchical feudal order. For example, in Weberian analysis lack of compatibility between capitalism and Confucianism was stressed. Though presently the opinions on their compatibility have been revised, but Confucianism's felicity with authoritarianism in the East Asian region is quite often asserted.

One can ascribe general ideas, which are common to Oriental societies, China has strong roots of such ideas. Like the idea of ethical values or individual perfection is one of the key beliefs of the Chinese public. But in this ethical ideas society has more importance than individual. That is, group be it family, society or state or monarchy occupy higher position. In political terms this translates into individual rights occupying no importance or lesser importance. As can be expected any such ideology, which stresses more importance on group or collective than individual rights, in practice inevitably, slides into respect for hierarchy. The respect for hierarchy gives supreme importance to leader. This cultural trait which is very much characteristic of Oriental civilizations, has strong roots in the Chinese politic. This attests to the Mao occupied supreme position. Most importantly, this importance to supreme leader arises from the precedence of collective over individual. As is generally the practice with the ideas which emphasizes group over individuals, may lead to the sacrifice of latter for former.

Another principle that comes out from primacy of society is of harmony *ren* which is one of the cardinal principles of Confucian philosophy. An ideal relationship between individual and the collective, between different principles leads to harmony. But the problem of principle of harmony is that it conceptualizes issues at the highest abstract level. The principle of harmony is emphasized in contemporary terms as well, for example Hu Jintao's principle of harmonious growth. But as is generally seen that the principle of harmony, is a matter of interpretation, and as interpreted by ruling elite. The ruling elite represent *li* in its different nuances. The term *li* means rites or decorum or process, which has to be consciously followed. This following of *li* at times acquires a situation of holding importance in form only. *Li* also represents a moral order, which is the substratum of the all happenings in the universe. One of the characteristic features of the Confucianism belief is their positive view of the human nature, which has to be perfected through following virtues. Further, the principle of *jen /ren* humanity or benevolence, which once again emphasizes the positive conception of human nature. The Chinese stress for the ritual propriety and cultivation of virtues under the sage king makes country's politics a large matter of passive acceptance.

The real import of the Confucius philosophy internationally is that it has extended in the neighbouring countries of Japan, Korea and Southeast Asia. The issue is not as much similarity of the views among the neighbouring countries, though by no means it is any less important. Yet the pressing question on China's political culture and /strategic culture will be the limits of the gaze. It is important that China's patient rise to a superpower status will provide it means to exercise its will. How this will is likely to express itself, is the moot point for China watchers. Though the present Chinese diplomacy talks of peaceful rise and harmonious growth. In fact many neighbouring countries have been a beneficiary of the Chinese principle of harmonious growth. This mutual economic interdependence has lead to China acquiring the epithet of being regions "economic locomotive". But as is the practice internally in the CCP ruled China the elites concept of harmony, has many losers domestically, with spawning of a middle level corrupt elite. The domestic developments do have international implications. Chinese concept of harmonious society will try to constraint other states policy options. Once, China does not have a need for positive appreciation of neighbouring countries, it is likely to put its weight behind its preferences.

The most important principle on which the political implication of Confucianism's stress on order harmony gives importance to the hierarchical world order, which makes the existing rulers, ruling through "mandate of heaven." The pervading belief of the

Confucianism where rulers rule through "mandate of heaven".[8] Confucianism's stress on order can be attributed as one of the reasons for people's passivity to the larger governmentality. Despite the perceived mounting challenges to state authority, as most strongly expressed in rising number of protests, the stability of the CCP is not under doubt. This is in part to beliefs of Confucianism guiding people's outlook. While the earlier tensions of state and society interaction especially over formers attempts to re-invent society in their image as in Cultural Revolution or Great Leap Forward Movement is no more present, rather a benign social contract exists between society is largely free to re-invent itself within the free market principles.

Any states cultural beliefs and practices are derived from two sources, one the principles they purport to follow, and the principles derived out from application of the principles. That is, when ideas have to be put into practise. But one of the characteristics of Chinese society is their attachment to absolute principles.[9] While attachment to absolute principles, may once again reflect strong adherence to *li* but may over a period of time slide into content less form.

While the historical legacy of Sinocentric world order, may be an accentuating factor for the regional states being a willing partners in Chinese growth strategy. Superpower China's diplomacy may have a different character. History of China has shown that they have not hesitated in interfering externally. While the Confucius system which at the same time asserts on ritual propriety that is *li* which as much guides the ASEAN way of diplomacy is unlikely to bind China or counter a belligerent China. In fact the Confucian principle of ritual propriety *li* may make China adhere to many regional security mechanisms, or practices as a passive actor. This may initially give the impression of China as passively peaceful but it is more to its predominant stress on ritual propriety. But once the interests began to change then therefore, gradually Chinese position on issues begin to shift. Thus, under a great deal of institutional paraphernalia and rhetoric China, shifts in position begin to take place. Thus at time we see a dual strategic culture, or a different interpretation of it.

The duality in the Chinese strategic culture is also due to its historical experiences. Chinese history of subjugation and domination has affected its culture and strategic outlook. It imparts an element of xenophobia, which is manifested even today over reaction to visits Yasukuni shrine in Japan. Due to its difficult history China comes over as a defensive nation with cautiousness in its external dealings. It explains many of the characteristic tendencies of the foreign policy like Dengist formulations like "lying low" and not taking leadership. The defensive element is very strong in the Chinese foreign and security policy. But according to Andrew Scobell maintains under "Chinese cult of defense", it practises a dual policy or dialectical policy.

The country's strategic culture, apart from its Confucian tradition is affected by its struggle against feudalism and Japanese imperialism. A particular tendency of victimhood at the hands of the external forces is a strong influence on country's self-image and external outlook. China sees its history as a century of humiliation. This victim mentality gives China defensive orientation but it also gives it characteristic inside/ outside outlook. By inside/outside outlook that is though they have suspicion and reserve over external actors, but it does not preclude them from holding strong linkages with outside actors.

As, the modern nation is formed from communist movement, which places emphasis on "war of position" and ideological flexibility. Where ideology is justified by the goal of people's revolution. It is ideological flexibility, which makes it possible for the Chinese government to support such rogue regimes like North Korea, Myanmar, Iran and Sudan. Further, the communist movement history gives its policy an element of militant streak, the country even though regularly emphasising its defensive nature is more than willing to use force in favour of its position. As Alastair Iain Johnston maintains Chinese have a *parabellum* strategic culture. According to Johnston,

> *parabellum* paradigm, assumes that conflict is a constant feature of human affairs, that it is due to largely to the rapacious or threatening nature of the adversary, that in this zero-sum context the application of violence is highly efficacious for dealing with the enemy. These assumptions generally translate into preference for offensive strategies followed by progressively less coercive ones, where accommodation is ranked last. There is some ambiguity at the most coercive end of this ranking whether "offensive" means expansionist or annexationist, or can include offensive use of forces within an active defense posture.[10]

This use of force is not only in response to a direct military threat but can also involve pre-emptive strike ostensibly defensive in nature. As the communist struggle predominantly relies on stratagem, it is also evident in its foreign and security policy. Though making great deal about the vouchsafed positions, they have an amazing flexibility. As in the Sino-Soviet relations while they were on the same side of ideological divide, after the split China began to form relationship with United States. China has patiently built United States for its bilateral relations.

Huiyun Feng, on Chinese strategic culture gives prime importance to the Confucian beliefs on inert-state relations. Author argues that, "Although *wu* (war, force or military) was always important in history as well, the dominance of *wen* (civilization or culture) documentation of stratagems and tactics rather than the bloody depiction of different wars and battles< that is, words of minds rather than deeds, shows pacific Chinese strategic and military preferences despite constant external threats from minorities in the border areas."[11] Feng takes the help of Confucian beliefs to argue that Chinese have a unique strategic culture and a pacific one she points out primary three reasons in attestation of its belief, one Confucian and Mencian injunctions which condemn violence.

Second, stress on defensive character. The Great Wall of China is seen as one of the prime examples of China's defensive outlook. She argues, China's defensiveness can be seen from the world-famous Great Wall built during the Warring Sates period (403-221BC), and until the Ming Dynasty (1368-1644), it was the defensive forefront against outside aggression. [12] Third, tradition of righteous war, or defensive war.

(ii) Military Thought

China's military strategy is important vis-a- vis strategic culture/ outlook. As China reassesses its place and role, its military strategy /doctrine has also begun to show the requisite change from people's war to people's war under modern conditions, and local war under hi tech conditions to local wars under the conditions of informationaistaion. China's attempt to match up with the most modern principles of defence preparedness shows that states do not exist in vacuum but are conscious exercisers of options.

This shift is also reflecting in China's transformation from a poor insecure nation to a military modern nation. People's war was a reflection of the Communism, at the same time it was also a reflection of its military weakness, where lack in asymmetric military power was to be made up through bigger number of the people. Therefore, the guerrilla tactics of communist revolutionary wars was to be employed, through such principles as 'luring enemy into deep'. Or the guerrilla warfare techniques was more geared towards fighting asymmetric war, but it was far from just being a defensive strategy. It involved a strong offensive strategy, by which the enemy will be conquered.[13] There are three stages of the people's war. In the first stage, "the protracted war begins with a strategic retreat or 'luring the enemy in deep.'"[14] Here the enemy strategy will be to follow the guerrilla tactics as propounded by Mao Tse Tung, "the enemy advances we retreat; the enemy camps, we harass; the enemy tires we attack; the enemy retreats we pursue."

In the second stage, both the parties will consolidate their respective advantages. "At this level, essentially one of stalemate, the disparity in the balance of forces is minimised. The 'weak army' has armed itself with an arsenal; captured from the 'strong', ruptured adversary morale, and mobilised the masses against the enemy.[15] And finally, the guerrilla forces in a regular war defeat the enemy forces.

In the contemporary times people's war seems not to be of any use, it has passed its significance. Militarily it may be of little use but as an ideological influence it still pervades as one of the legacies of Maoist thought. More importantly, the peoples war concept imparts tenacity to Chinese military outlook and it also imparts a characteristic brinkmanship attitude to its strategic outlook. As people's war is a total war, it makes people expendable collateral in the larger war. Therefore, Chinese support for rogue regimes is understandable, more importantly its tendency to be cruel to one's own people is derived from its ideological pre-disposition. Also, China being able to absorb nuclear threat, and yet survive derives from the same thinking. As in case of Chinese willingness to use threat of nuclear weapons in case of Taiwan crisis also has its genesis in Maoist concept of people's war.

As Rosita Dellios maintains:

> We have observed that the genre to which people's war belongs is independent of the need for large professional armies. This characteristic may not be useful to the defence requirements of a modern nation state, but it may prove to be a vital survival quality if the specialised military functions of a victim society are effectively destroyed. In the hypothetical post-nuclear battlefield of the future, so long as there are surviving populations amenable to organised resistance, people's war might prove an ideal, or perhaps the only possible strategy against an occupation force.[16]

People's war under modern conditions was recognition of the need for the technological modernisation of the army, which instead of relying on its weakness, should rather aim to develop a professional military. While Segal maintains that the " people's war is pre-eminently a notion of military science – a concept like Communism itself that is so general as to set basic goals but not serve as a blueprint for day-today action. People's war has some impact on military art, but it is at this, more pragmatic level that China's 'modern conditions' has a greater impact. People war must have popular support and be suited to local conditions."[17] It is in the latter aspect that the war must have popular support, which has made military a follower of CCP, than policy arbiter. Though, in the present circumstances Maoist Peoples War remains a misnomer, but its legacy in terms of popular support endures.

If the people's war was making virtue out of necessity, then people's war under modern conditions was a response to the changing conditions. Now the PLA were unlike Red Army relying on man to defeat the machine. But rather it was a status-quoist force which had gradually built up a war fighting machinery. According to Nan Li there are five major differences between people's war and the people's war under modern conditions.[18] Firstly, rather than drawing the enemy into interiors, now they were to be fought at borders. Secondly, now early battles were more important that protracted wars of attrition. Thirdly, now the positional warfare was as important as earlier mobile warfare. Fourthly, now cities were to be defended as against earlier dictum of retreat to rural areas. Fifthly, now the old dictum of victory by denial was to be supplemented by deterrence through retaliation.

In the people's war under modern conditions the imperative for a professional military was increasingly being felt. PLA's business ventures began to wind down. Further, in mid-1980s China embarked on reduction of PLA by a million. Now the focus was turning to from strength in numbers to technological superiority. The most important change in Chinese military strategy was derived from the Gulf War of 1991. Further, the Gulf War was forcing China to revisit its military options and strategy, the quick rout of famed Iraq Revolutionary Guards made China to take a re-look. US displayed an array of hi-tech weapons that led to the China reassessing its military modernisation. The need for Revolution in Military Affairs had hit China hard. Also, the focus was on the future wars, it was being realised that future wars will not be total wars as envisaged under the Maoist people's war. It would be now local or limited wars, involving clash at borders as it may happen in case of Taiwan. Even the use of nuclear weapons was unlikely; rather it will involve a missile war.

Chinese concept of local wars is in distinction to total wars, local wars may not be necessarily a minor war. According to Pillsbury, "local war is understood to be a limited war on the periphery of

China that should be short but intense, utilizing advanced technology weapons, with units fighting in a joint and combined arms effort. It envisions an element of force projection (the ability to transport combat forces beyond China's borders), but by definition is regional, not global."[19]

The most important far reaching change was that a gradual move from defensive orientation to offensive posture was taking place. That is, China will have to focus on force projection, which with its various concomitant effects is going to produce a regional security dynamic. In fact, the regional countries are concerned about China's military modernisation and objectives. "As the PLA's focus of war preparation is shifting from the 'three norths' to east and south China, the group armies in the strategic force are constantly engaged in long-range manoeuvres in the southern military regions."[20] This re-look is in line with the realisation that China's strategic frontiers exist beyond its geographical boundaries. Especially as China's economic interest widen, safeguarding SLOCs (Sea Line of Communication) become a dominant imperative. Therefore, what we see is that Chinese strategic culture or outlook do not just rest with traditional ideas and practices, they are being influenced by modern developments. As, China has taken steps towards inclusion in the global system, concomitantly its strategic frontiers have widened. Earlier goal was to wage a defensive war, now the force projection and out of area contingency operations become necessary for China.

In the domain of discussion about future wars, the local war had two variants, earlier one was the local wars under hi-tech conditions which was announced in 2004 defence white paper, it was later re-named as the local wars under conditions of informationaisation. Under both the Chinese leadership both political and military is aware of the need for a lean and mean military machine. It had to incorporate new developments in technology which compose various aspects of C4ISR. Accordingly stress on cyber and space wars, in both the context China has taken active lead. It is in the later aspects, which China's military modernisation is leading to the apprehensions world wide. As Kevin Pollpeter, "...Chinese writers describe space systems as important to the conduct of war and assert that in future wars China must first gain mastery of space before it can cope for victory on earth."[21] The important point to note once again is that China's reference point is United States. That is they are in security dynamic which feed on each other, as "the perception that space warfare is inevitable and that the US military is highly vulnerable to strikes against its space system may not be only one factor that leads China to attack US space assets, but also may lead them to believe that they can conduct a successful military campaign against the United States."[22]

The real import of China's military modernisation is that even if a debate on the Chinese strategic culture may remain inconclusive, but a competing system of military modernisation may spiral out of control or may make use of military instruments a viable policy. But in case of China which had an offensive strategic culture, with a history to attest this, it is likely that military modernisation and development will pose a problem for the regional security. As, "China's past success in assessing and modulating the risks it was running may give it confidence that it will be able to do so in the future as well."[23]

Table 2.1

China's Military Expenditure

Year	% of GDP*	Defence Expenditure $*	% of GDP#	Defence Expenditure RMB	Percentage of Government Expenditure
1999	1.8	21.6	1.2	107.640	8.16
2000	1.8	23.8	1.22	120.754	7.60
2001	2.0	28.5	1.32	144.204	7.63
2002	2.1	33.4	1.42	170.778	7.74
2003	2.1	36.4	1.40	190.787	7.74
2004	2.1	40.6	1.38	220.001	7.72
2005	2.0	44.9	1.35	247.496	7.29
2006	2.0	52.2	1.41	297.938	7.37
2007	2.0	57.9	1.38	355.491	7.14
2008		63.6			
2009					

Source: SIPRI Year Book 2009

 # Chinese Government Figures available in White Paper http://www.china.org.cn/government/central_government/2009-01/20/content_17155577_21.htm

(iii) State/ Society Pressures

Another characteristic, which emerges out of Chinese communist tradition, is that people/society play an important part in its foreign policy imaginings. This societal focus, makes them very critical of outside comments on internal matters of China, but it also makes them less interfering in other country's affairs. Therefore, principle of sovereignty is a cardinal virtue, which is to be followed. This does not follows from some universal principles, but right of society to re-invent themselves or to put in Communist slogans, right to revolution. This would have been more applicable under Mao reign. But this holds true for the Dengist period as well, though in a communist state people have more duty to revolution than right to revolution. But in the post Mao period duty to revolution was to be exercised through unleashing people's entrepreneurial talent. But the overarching framework was the same. This they had to do under the overall framework of Communist tutelage. Thus pro-democracy demonstration at Tiananmen Square in 1989, had no other option but was to be crushed. All foreign relations were to be seen in this context, providing material withal to advance productivity. This obsession with ones society has twin implications, a major part of the Communist elites attention is forced within, that is its outward gaze is limited. As Chinese history points out major attempts to re-invent society have been a failure. Thus, perhaps now the Chinese society and politics will be more focused on regulative aspects. That is man in order and in society therefore, aspects like censoring of google etc. continues to be important. While this withdrawal from active efforts in interpreting society leaves elite with sufficient time to look internationally, which China has taken to perfection. But this withdrawal from active efforts in re-inventing society does not solve the state society equation. That is, legitimacy questions will always be there, though the Confucian ideal of obedience to authority is important. But the communist elite of the state and society will be in unstable equilibrium, which may rapidly deteriorate. This disjuncture can lead to elites being autonomous, but in reality it characterises that lack of people behind the government. This is ambiguous for CCP peoples approval required is congenital, but it can be double-edged. Thus, China even if it likes to take more global role it will always be constrained by its state-society vulnerability. That is it cannot be as sure of public opinion backing it as other democracies like United States United Kingdom and India. Thus, China even if it becomes global power or superpower its gaze is likely to be restricted regionally. But with the larger autonomy from societal matters may propel China toward military adventurism. It will depend on a host of factors, but chances are likely that military modernisation will give China an added incentive to use force.

This translates into strong rhetoric of anti-colonialism and multi-polar world. As ultimately its foreign policy is justified to common people not to any standards of international behaviour. Positively, it could mean as Johnston talks of another strand of strategic culture in China which in contrast to *parabellum* culture is Confucian-Mencian paradigm, "assumes essentially that conflict is aberrant or at least avoidable through the promotion of good government and the co-opting or enculturation of external threats."[24] However, even in case of Confucian-Mencian paradigm force can be used, but this can be done only by first exhausting all means of accommodation, resultantly the force used should be minimal and defensive in orientation, until the moral political order is restored. But in these two competing strands of strategic culture the former *parabellum* strategic culture predominates.

China can take any steps in this belief. With no democracy in the country the slogan of the people ultimately boils down to the interpretation of the peoples wishes, which is finally interpreted by the communist elite, who have the twin roles of representatives of the peoples as well as their leaders. In the end, the Chinese Communist Party can go to any extremes in the name of people's policy. It can also ruthlessly crush a student's movement for democracy as happened in the Tiananmen in 1989. As very well exemplified in this case the recourse to people imparts Chinese policy a self -righteousness impervious to popular opinions.

Another very dominant feature of the Chinese strategic imaginations is its historical lineage of great power belief. China is an ancient civilisation, which had achieved great material and cultural progress with influence extending over neighbouring countries in East Asia and South East Asia. This is a strong Chinese strategic belief but it's needed to be studied in conjunction with a century of shame and humiliation. These claims to great power heritage also become a means of propaganda and a reality denying mechanism. China's obsession to re-claim its great power heritage. In its ancient glory it has seen itself to be a middle kingdom, which owe a special degree of obligation. This belief seeing China as middle kingdom also imparts China an inside/outside outlook. The belief in middle kingdom with contiguous territories owing a special obligation is a not a reflection of inward self-satisfied nation as was the case with India. Despite Indian trade and cultural outlook spreading across the region from West Asia to South East Asia, it north Indian view has been inward looking, insular and self-absorbent. In contrast, to sea faring culture of South India, where many expedition had taken place in South East Asia.

But in the various studies of strategic culture the role of society as a repository of culture of ages is emphasised. And also a clear distinction of state and society is maintained, but the need for state in society perspective is needed.[25] In our search for strategic culture we only give society a secondary importance as in providing ideas into social practice. Further, it tends to reify or essentialise culture and somehow gives it a position of stationariness with giving more than important role for the society's history. Therefore, the state in society approach will give strategic culture a more dynamic importance, as it is likely state-in-society have no settled relationship, but continuous duel. As in Marxist literature society is very important, in fact in the communist utopia, the state will wither away. It has been a theoretical injunction, and has not practically taken place. But in case of Maoist China, their has been a continuous duel, where states have tried to make society in their image through two mass movements of Great Leap Forward and Cultural Revolution. These movements have also been called purges, inflicting misery on the Chinese public. As Shue emphasises, "the new minted party state then took as its first and most important task nothing less than reinventing Chinese society."[26] Both attempts have drastically failed, but they also immeasurably changed the state-society relationship. "State society engagement by these means had thus tended to become a ritualized matter. And in the Cultural Revolution what we finally witnessed was the nearly complete disjuncture of state rhetoric and social action."[27] Shue further argues that "the real power of the party -state apparatus to mobilize society was by then seriously eroded. And the real power dispersed throughout society was deeply parcelized and nearly exhausted in phony political struggles."[28] Attempts have been made to rectify this imbalance, which according to Shue has resulted in new intermediate level arenas of state-society relation." But if such a trend toward convergence of state power and social organisation at the intermediate levels of the polity is now actually under way in China, it still remains to be seen whether (and how precisely) this trend proves empowering for newly organized social interest."[29] In fact, Shue's assertion of intermediate level of state-society interaction has been manifested in Chinese foreign policy practice as well. China has been taking this approach in developing a regional interdependence approach with the neighbouring countries. Be it through development of regional infrastructure or interdependent economic groupings like GMS. GMS is the most important example because in the Chinese representation has been taken by Yunan. Further, the Kunming initiative, in which the Chinese state of Yunan was the key participant, was formed. After the death of Mao in 1976 a diminution in state-society relations have taken place, Both due to absence of charismatic personality like Mao and the belief by Deng Xiaoping that Maoist policies have led to mass starvation and social upheaval.

Means: Spectral or Multilayered Approach

One of the characteristic approaches of the Chinese strategic practice is what can be called spectral approach. Though, it can be said that countries under the Waltzian structure have to conform to the systemic pressures in terms of instruments exercised in the advancing states interests. But if studies of strategic culture have to have any meaning then they have to concede nation's cultural specificities. Like India even under the constraining pressures of the bipolar world, was able to stay away from the group power politics, and ingeniously devised a third way of non-alignment. This was very specific to its strategic culture of looking world in moral order terms.

It can be said that almost all nation states advance their nation states security interests through all the possible means, military, diplomatic, economic, and ideological. China is no exception either. But China's strategic culture has a special knack for discourse domination, whose felicity cannot be seen as much in other countries strategic practice.[30] The use of discourses in advancing nation states interest is different from ideological approach. While the ideological approach tends to project one country's best image and policies, so as to lead to what in the modern parlance is called "soft power" approach. The Chinese felicity to use words and phrases is also intrinsic to peculiarities of Chinese language. A necessary element of duality or ambiguity or contradictoriness is there in key doctrines and phrases.

These ambiguities are not just inherent to the Chinese language but also are a means of built in deception. Thus they can claim a leeway not only as a direct concession arising out of negotiation but also claim to be misinterpreted. This gives them in accepting a less beneficial position because of subordinate position. But due to its special felicity for ambiguity, it can challenge the decision in future. As has happened in case of standards accepted for settling boundary between India and China, which accepted that status of settled population will not be altered. It was later rescinded by China.

It is due to the spectral multidimensional and multilayered characteristic of China where every issue is linked and related, it is difficult to arrive at a closure. Therefore, China simultaneously calls for opposition of hegemony in international relations, (countering United States dominance in international relations), while at the same time building one of the closest relations with United States. It is this spectral outlook that one is linked to other, where almost all things are interlinked. Steve Chan, also asserts that Chinese 'statecraft is multidimensional and involves opposing injunctions or bimodal reasoning (e.g., to be bold *and* cautious, to bluff strength *and* to feign weakness, to be patient *and* to be opportunistic). As a matter of comparison with standards U.S. strategic thinking, however, it is likely to assume that a state's power trajectory will be characterized by a linear progression. Instead, the Chinese are likely to take a dialectic or cyclical view of the waning and waxing of national power."[31] Hence, it is difficult to get easy settlements on key issues. That is everything falls under the one continuum. It is inevitable as well where institutionalisation has not taken place due to communism. All things are interlinked. For example, China advanced new security concept in 1996, which called for, "mutual trust, mutual benefit, equality and coordination" among countries.[32] It contains laudable normative principles like desisting from cold war mentality, power politics and advancing security through cooperation and dialogue. The new security concept makes a mention of the Asia-Pacific region. It also mentions on expanding concept of security, it says "under the new historical conditions, the meaning of the security concept has evolved to be multifold with its contents extending from military and political to economic, science and technology, environment, culture and many other areas."[33] While on level it can be said that it has emphasised on the widening of the concept, but it also reminds of the inter-relatedness of the security. Though it may point to the contemporary developments in the field of security studies, but Chinese strategic culture zero sum view, implies an unyielding view as evident in Mekong riparians complaints over its dam building spree. As, Hong notes that in Chinese concept "the elements of traditional and non-traditional threats to security are intertwined".[34] If this is so it implies that Chinese state behaviour even in these issues, will look for relative gains and dominant position, even though new concept of security talks against "one sided security", it is likely that once its grand strategy of peaceful rise is achieved, it will revert to one-sided security focusing on relative gains.

China's Contemporary Grand Strategy

China can be said to be following four general principles of grand strategy.[35] Foremost is the Chinese desire to reclaim great power status. This is one aspect, which is central to the Chinese foreign policy practice and self–image. In other words, this aspiration is put forward as the middle kingdom complex. The self-image of a great power is not only a persistent tradition of considerable historical lineage but also reflected in almost obsessive practice of postulating foreign policy choices with reference to the United States. China is making rapid strides in achieving this great power status, alternatively termed as "peaceful rise" or "peaceful development." The puzzle around which the future of Asian geopolitics is discussed is whether it will be Asia's China or China's Asia.[36] Asia will be the primary theatre of this geopolitical contest, as despite the pretensions of being a global power, China is quintessentially a regional actor. When we assert that China is essentially a regional actor, it is not intention to agree with Gerald Segal's rhetorical question, "Does China Matter?"[37] Rather, China will essentially seek to dominate Asia-Pacific.

Second, cardinal principle of the Chinese grand strategy is the necessity for a peaceful international environment, in which economic progress can be pursued. This is the core of Chinese exhortation to follow "peaceful development." Chinese elite recognise the centrality of the economic progress without which the ambitions of becoming a great power cannot be realised. Economic development not only provides the necessary material withal to provide for the impoverished people, but also requisite finance to proceed with the military modernisation. China has very devotedly followed this policy without fail. Also, it seems to have taken a lesson from the defeat of the Soviet Union in the Cold War, which was owing to the Soviet Unions domestic economic difficulties. China has managed to steadfastly cling to this policy even in situations of grave provocation like the Belgrade bombing of its embassy by the United States in May 1999, though the United States claimed the bombing was accidental, yet Chinese were skeptical of the US claim, and believed this to a be a deliberate act of upmanship. Despite the public protests over the incident, and seeming possibility of China taking a vehement anti-US posture in the international relations. Chinese elite refrained from shifting the gears. The economic constituent of the grand strategy got a fillip with China getting an entry into World Trade Organisation in 2001.

Third, very often cited Dengist claims of not seeking leadership. Analysts generally call this as a principle proscribing pre-mature leadership, which China cannot afford. And finally, the recognition that China is in an interdependent world where its policy formulations have to recognise this aspect as well. This paper will argue that China is maintaining the traditional core principles of its grand strategy, but it has begun to take a more nuance and active part in the geo-strategic calculus of the region. Though, China has global ambitions, yet primarily it is proactive regionally. On the global level it espouses multi-polarity in the international system. China, while at the same time maintaining "constructive strategic partnership" with United States, it actively calls for a multi-polar world order. This point specially comes out in joint foreign policy declarations coming out of the summit meeting, with powers like Russia. The core of the Chinese grand strategy constitutes in its desire for a multi-polar world and unipolar Asia. It is difficult to say that this will be one of the realistic objectives of the Chinese grand strategy. However, Russian grand strategy will be in conflict with its dual location, that is, both in Asia and Europe, with inclination more towards the European continent. Chinese analysts believe that time is on their side, and their key objective is to exploit the opportunities, without incurring any substantive obligations.

The fourth principle of its grand strategy flows from the third, where China recognizes that it is a part of an interdependent world, whose untroubled functioning is in its self-interest. This explains why China has been a cooperative actor in the 1997 Asian financial crisis, when it refused to devalue its currency. This was one incident where China managed an image makeover. It was able to convey an image of the responsible stakeholder in the functioning of the international system. Chinese grand strategy has been to exploit the "unipolar moment" in the international system. The unipolarity not only imparted political prudence, where it consciously refrained from acting openly against the predominant power of the United States. Even it felt that US has been provocative enough in the 1999 bombing of its embassy in the Belgrade or EP-3 spy plane incident. However, at the same time it has managed to exploit the unipolarity to the hilt by free riding the system, which very remarkably manifested in its joining of the WTO in 2001, which led to the tremendous increase in its global trade. As Chong-pin Lin, argue that "Beijing's grand strategy is based on the belief that time is on China's side, and at present, it is unwise to confront the United States militarily or to force unification with Taiwan."[38] As, Goldstein maintains, "Beijing saw strategic partnership with the US as a way to cope with the potentially dangerous constraints of American hegemony during China's rise to great power status."[39]

According to Swaine and Tellis, the Chinese grand strategy is *calculative strategy* where "the notion of "calculative" strategy is defined in *substantive* terms as a pragmatic approach that emphasizes the primacy of internal economic growth and stability, the nurturing of amicable international relations, the relative restraint in the use of force combined with increasing efforts to create a more modern military, and the continued search for asymmetric gains internationally."[40]

China's Grand Strategy and Asia-Pacific

The neo-realists and realists earlier argued that the "unipolar moment" will be a transitionary period, either leading to bipolarity or multi-polarity, that is, post cold war is nothing but a "unipolar illusion".[41] Nearly two decade has passed since this prediction was made, yet no serious and direct threat to the US primacy has come about. The country, which is generally said to be challenging the US primacy, is China. However, China in its major policy pronunciations and practise, has made it clear that it is not going to enter into any sort of hard balancing against US. Or in Deng's formulation, it is biding for the right time. In grand strategic terms, Chinese policy is termed as "economic pre-balancing". [42]According to Layne, ""Economic pre-balancing" occupies a middle ground between soft balancing and hard balancing. States that pursue economic pre-balancing are trying to avoid the risks of engaging in premature arms build-up aimed at the United States by concentrating first on closing the economic and technological gap between them and the United States."[43] This paper argues that China in Asia-Pacific is following a policy of "*concessionary balancing*," where China recognises that its prime region of influence is Asia-Pacific.[44] Concessionary Realism is used to describe inter-state relations, as distinct from realism and neorealism. Sanders, get to concessional realism, in "thought experiment which attempts to specify what neo-realism and neo-liberalism might look like if their efforts to constitute rational choice theory were substantially downgraded. Concessional realism, "implies a much more direct focus on the problems of categorising and identifying national and transnational "interests". It focuses on "a wider range of "real" instances of foreign policy decision making."

Though, US has declared that it would not allow any "peer competitor" to arise to challenge its global dominance. But US has come to realise that it is under some sort of "imperial overstretch" being involved in Middle East.[45] Further, owing to the rapid economic progress and concerted drive for military modernisation China is estimated to become a first rate military power by 2020. The American primacy will be difficult to maintain if not entirely overtaken or challenged by some revisionist power thus US policy circles are discussing alternative plans for countering Chinese threat. But the real challenge is that China will take all measures to see that it doesn't antagonise US, even though symbolically taking on US, as in Copenhagen or Obama's visit to China. This is also a reluctant recognition of the fact that twin choices of containment and engagement has not been successful. Rather, China has defeated them in their own game using engagement to end isolation and build diplomatic trust. On the other hand, using containment to build an alternative pole so to speak around which anti-US states can be grouped or mobilized. In this case, its special relationship with the so-called rogue states is a case in point. China has made appropriate noises to show their support. Yet, at the same time refraining from going all the way in their support. Now as it has managed to bring the so-called rogue states in its sphere of influence it has begun to nudge them in the direction of the international public opinion or practising "China's new dictatorship diplomacy."[46]

Why it is concessionary?

The Oxford Dictionary defines concession as a thing granted or conceded.[47] Chinese characteristic foreign policy in Asia-Pacific can be called concessionary because, the aim of its grand strategy is that concessions are conceded or granted by both bigger powers and smaller powers, under an overall medley of instruments of power both soft and hard power. Hence the region is likely to concede China the status of eminent power, not as spoils of war, but as a means of superior power. Here the superior status is given as a grant, the region is known for historically owing a sense of tributary to the Chinese. The concessionary balancing allows for cultural specificity of Chinese style of power and regions history. As Medeiros, says Chinese power is "more gravitational than confrontational."[48] It is concessionary as against soft power approach, because, calculation of relative power weight is essential in giving concessions and grants. While soft power approach likes to exercise power by attraction.[49] But in concessionary balancing, relative power is an essential element of concession or balancing. Asia-Pacific despite high rates of growth continues to witness high arms expenditure. The Chinese policies are concessionary because they are not only seeking concessions but also giving concessions as well. Here smaller states will like grant from the bigger powers. Despite the much muscle flexing between China and United States, it is unlikely that China will be a global policemen as the United States is, therefore in these two powers an element of cooperation will always exist due to their different outlook. In fact in the recent Sino-US Joint Statement released over Obama's visit to China US gave China a position of overseer. Chinese have a long diplomatic practice and culture of seeking concessions from the major powers. Despite the public acceptance of the Deng's 24 character of not seeking leadership China has in the last two years worked actively to concede to the West's demand on sensitive issues like North Korea, Myanmar, Sudan and Iran. This recognition of the fact they are an integral element of the rapidly globalising and interdependent world very resolutely manifested itself in the 1997 Asian financial crisis, where they managed to convey an image of a responsible stakeholder in the international politics. Very notable has been going from the last two years further it must be noted that the earlier Chinese dictum of refraining from leadership was partly derived from the recognition that China is distrusted even in its own neighbourhood owing to the export of Maoist insurgency in the neighbourhood in the 1960s and 1970s. Now its status in the neighbourhood has begun to change as very well encapsulated in the Shambaugh's statement "China's neighbours are increasingly looking to Beijing for regional leadership or at a minimum they are taking account of China's interests and concerns. China's own diplomacy has grown more confident, omni-directional and proactive; its economy is now a major engine of regional growth; its military is steadily modernizing; and its regional posture is increasingly seen as benign"[50]

One of the big tickets to "great power exceptionalism" was given by the West, where China was given the permanent membership of the United Nations Security Council, only developing country to get it. The permanent membership not only imparts status and prestige to China but also it has also provided China tremendous leverage in Security Council deliberations. This explains why China is not in favour of expanding Security Council, as its expansion is most likely to get its two Asia-Pacific competitors India and Japan. China has at times used this leverage to bail out its close friends as it did in the January 2007 where it vetoed punitive Security Council Resolution against Myanmar. Though China has used veto sparingly about six times but under veto threat it has been able to exercise sufficient leverage over friends and allies It won't be an overstatement to argue the permanent membership is biggest concession given by West particularly US to help in realise China's great power ambitions.

The other major concession given by the West in its rise is the opportunity to economically develop. However, the intention is not to argue that the all the Chinese economic modernization and progress can be attributed to the West. Rather, it cannot be overlooked that the Chinese economic progress in large part owes to the West's active cooperation. West's contribution to the Chinese economic rise has been phenomenal. In fact, it has led some analysts to argue that US has been underwriting China's rise. Sino-US trade deficit is to the extent of more than $80 billion. The Sino-US trade deficit has become a permanent feature of their trade balances. Whereas earlier the focus was on the trade deficit between US and Japan now the focus has shifted to Sino-US trade deficit which according to Layne " is a de-facto American subsidy of the very economic growth that is fueling China's great power emergence."[51]

There are analysts who argue that more and more Chinese integration into the Western liberal economic order will constrain the revisionist impulses of China. This is the crux position of the engagement advocates.[52] They want to avoid the self-fulfilling prophecy of the containment theorists. The grand strategists who argue from the US perspective about the engagement as one of the policy options, is regarded by the realists both from the US and Chinese perspective as "internal balancing" or "economic prebalancing" or in Deng's terms as "biding our time". Wang argues that China is practicing "internal balancing" and "external soft balancing." He points out " the strategy of internal balancing entails accelerated economic growth and military modernisation that emphasizes asymmetric strategies whereas the strategy of soft balancing calls for joining and even creating multilateral institutions and engaging in "great power diplomacy" (*daguo waijiao*)."[53] In this debate internal balancing and engagement one aspect is generally glossed over that Chinese economic development is very much a product of concessionary balancing where concessions are consciously and purposely sought and with equal awareness and deliberation concessions are granted. That is, concessions are negotiated from both the sides. This is, especially applicable in the context of Sino-US trade. The most important thing to be noted in concessionary balancing is that the interests of the sole superpower and emerging power China are not as antithetical to each other, as is generally assumed it to be.

Sino - US trade relations have acquired a very strong dynamic presently, have also contributed to the Chinese gradual accession into the world trading system. In this context, China, which was pursuing a policy of "peaceful rise," negotiated very patiently to secure and maintain trade relations. In the early 1990s, China was under the continuous threat of US withdrawing MFN (Most Favoured Nation) status, which would have adversely affected its trade surplus. In this case both the countries very doggedly negotiated for concessions from both side. US wanted reduction in tariffs and non-tarriff barriers, while China wanted the end of annual review of the Congress for the MFN status. The annual review would generally put the spotlight on China's human rights record, which China detested. To end this annual review China and US signed a trade agreement in November 1999, which paved the way for Chinese entry into WTO in 2001. In pursuit of this agreement Permanent Normal Trade Relations (PNTR) China made "significant compromises."[54] Copeland maintains that "the Chinese leadership understood that without such concessions it could not achieve two core goals: the ending of the annual review by Congress of China's most favoured nation status; and the forging of Washington's support for China's entry into the WTO."[55] After WTO accession the Chinese world trade got a big fillip as the trade data statistics speak for itself. However, it must be emphasized that in this case both sides have conceded and gained from the agreement.

This "concessionary balancing" can very well be discerned in China's behaviour in security relations as well. China realises that stable Sino-US relations is central to its great power diplomacy. Even though it does opposes unipolarity in the international system. In its *Defense White Paper* "the world is at a critical stage going toward multi-polarity."[56] Yet, it takes adequate care not to be seen as the "peer competitor "of the only superpower. Rather, it has taken the advise of the Deputy Secretary of State Robert Zoellick calling for China to become a "responsible stakeholder" in the international system. This statement from the US official was not only a warning to China to temper its stance towards the so-called rogue states. But also a grudging acceptance of the "imperial overstretch" in Middle East and Afghanistan and US needed China's help in managing the recalcitrant states of the international system. In this mutual concession one thing is especially notable for the powers of Asia, is that regional spheres of influence might be mutually agreed upon. This is, very likely in the case of US and China rather signs of this happening are already coming to the fore and US has begun to accept as pointed in latest policy journal *Foreign Affairs* that "the United States's "unipolar moment" will inevitably end."[57] A grand strategy that is increasingly popular in security analysts in United States is "offshore balancing." This strategy involves that "the United States should deploy military power abroad only in the face of direct threats to vital American interests. The strategy recognises that Washington need not (and in fact cannot) directly control vast parts of the globe, that, it is better off setting priorities that based on clear national interests and relying on local actors to uphold regional balances of power."[58] Further, "the idea of an offshore balancing strategy is to get the United States out of China's crosshairs not to allow it to remain a target because of its present security commitments to allies in the region."[59] The fear is that US grand strategy of "offshore balancing" and Chinese grand strategy of "concessionary balancing" will lead to China dominating Asia-Pacific. As Christopher Layne argues " the wisdom of risking war with China to maintain US hegemony in East Asia is all the more doubtful because America's predominance is ebbing in any event by pulling back from its hegemonic role in East Asia and adopting an offshore balancing strategy the United States could better preserve its relative power and influence."[60] Contrary to the general belief that US and China are having irreconcilable relations especially in the East Asia is not very well borne out in reality. In fact in 2001, Chinese Foreign Minister Tang Jiaxuan made the statement that China sees US presence in the Asia-Pacific as a stabilizing factor. In fact, China specialist Shambaugh draws a long list of 35 thirty-five regional issues concerning Asia. Of these on sixteen issues China and US are in convergence on eight issues they diverge and eleven issues they are uncertain.[61] China's positive appreciation of the US role in Asia-Pacific is significant when we compare that China took active lead in its progenitor organisation Shanghai Cooperation Organisation (SCO) calling for withdrawal of the US troops from Central Asia. This is significant, though in Central Asia it has energy needs but it is also aware that and at times openly accepting that it is free riding from the strategic benign environment engendered from the US's role as global policemen. This is characteristic Chinese practice of diversionary practice of raising issues to divert the US' attention from China's gradual spread of influence in Asia-Pacific while making it as Central Asia is slipping out of the US control. In the Astana Summit in 2005, SCO asked US troops to withdraw from the Central Asia. US did lose its military base in Uzbekistan and was bargaining for the other base in Kyrgystan. SCO is generally regarded in the West as anti-US. In short, China is trying to balance US in Central Asia and cooperate in the Asia-Pacific, which is its prime region of influence. It is not to state that Central Asia is unimportant for China but only to assert that China is deliberately upping the ante in Central Asia as "New Great Game" while surreptitiously shoring up its influence in Asia-Pacific. As a scholar from Shanghai Institute of International Studies maintains that "from the Chinese there is also a kind of worry that the United States would use the war of anti-terrorism to come to Central Asia and contain China's strategic space there. However, the SCO should not be an issue in Sino-US bilateral relationship. Both of the two countries still have chance to reshape the other's perception."[62]

China and Asia-Pacific Regionalism

China's attitude has fundamentally altered on participation in the regional security and non-security institutions. From the initial distrust of regional security institutions seeing it as an instrument of the US to check its rise to as a means of diminution of insecurity and anxiety of the neighbouring states. China has been especially very successful in engendering and exploiting the regional security and economic groupings. In fact, it is being regarded as the locomotive behind regions splendid economic growth. China has very successfully managed to convey its peaceful intention to its neighbours by participating in a plethora of regional organisations like ASEAN+1 (ASEAN and China) ASEAN+3 (ASEAN, China, Japan and South Korea), the ARF, the ASEAN Vision Group, the ASEAN Senior Officials Meetings and the Pacific Basin Economic Council. Then there is ASEM Asia-Europe Meeting. Coupled with this is the existence of a number of track two initiatives like CSCAP Council on Security Cooperation in the Asia-Pacific, the Northeast Asia Security Cooperation Dialogue, and the Shangri la Dialogue. Above it, China has launched two regional security initiatives on its own, firstly is the SCO and the Boao Forum which is a track two initiative organized by Chinese government where participants meet annually on Hainan island. China's involvement with the ASEAN is wide ranging and central to its "charm offensive" in Southeast Asia. China's and US's trade with ASEAN almost run parallel to each other but while the China has trade surplus of $178 billion with the world but it has a trade deficit with the ASEAN to the tune of $18 billion. In 2006 US trade with ASEAN was at $168.5 billion, while that of China was at $160.9 billion.[63] China and ASEAN have entered into a Free Trade Agreement in 2002, which will be the third largest free trade area in the world after NAFTA and EU. China and ASEAN have entered into a number of security arrangements as well like Declaration on Conduct in South China Sea (2002); the Joint Declaration on the Field of Non-traditional Security Issues (2002) and Joint Declaration on Strategic Partnership for Peace and Prosperity (2003). China's regional strategy has been very successful that even the US is willing to work with China in Southeast Asia. A recent report from *Congressional Research Servi*ce recommends to "establish a new dialogue process with China with the goal of reassuring China that the United States does not seek to counter China in Southeast Asia or to contain China more broadly...reinvigorating and expanding confidence building measures and other forms of engagement that seek to reassure China that the United States and its allies are not trying to contain China. It may be equally important to prevent China from adopting a strategic posture that would lead to strategic rivalry between the United States and China in the region and beyond."[64] China's regional diplomacy has been so successful that regional officials are claiming that China has displaced US in terms of influence, as very aptly put that "China fear" has been replaced by "China fever."[65] With China embarking on Greater Mekong Sub-region (GMS) the program is especially geared to involve landlocked countries of Southeast Asia. "China's aid to the Philippines was roughly four times greater than America's, China's aid to Laos was three times greater, its aid to Indonesia was nearly double, and its aid to Cambodia nearly matched US levels."[66]

Why it is balancing?

The most plausible reason for this is that China's self-image as great power will always impel it towards balancing. As already pointed out the East Asian region has been under the boundary of middle kingdom complex. Further, systemic analysis of international politics cannot ignore the attempts to carve out spheres of influence. Even though in a rapidly globalising world it may seem misnomer. Even though China has undertaken a concessionary balancing of the United States which can be very aptly helped by "off-shore balancing" of the United States. Yet, China continues to undertake massive military modernisation. Further, the power projection capability is further amplified by the fact of Chinese development in the infrastructure notably in Tibet. However, despite Chinese attempts to modernise its PLA it is essentially a defensive force with more oriented towards land based operations than having sea denial or air operations. Further, PLA Air Force (PLAAF) and PLA Navy (PLAN) are limited in their operational capabilities. Thus, it is in no position to match the technologically advanced air force and navy of Japan. That is, out of area operation capability is especially limited. Also, China is presently no match to hard power of United States yet estimates as done by US think tanks suggest that by 2020 China will be an advanced military power. Further, the issue around which military power will become central to the Sino-US diplomacy is the Taiwan issue. China resents military equipment provided to Taiwan by US. Also, China has not renounced use of force in case of Taiwan. US military presence is preponderant in Asia-Pacific not only through bilateral military alliances but also through its military base in Guam and Hawaii. But there has been an incident when China has worked under arm to limit the US policy options, as when Dennis Blair, US Commander in the Pacific, supported security communities with many Asian nations involving, defence cooperation, the Asian states rejected the idea on the prodding from China.[67]

The puzzle is around how will the rest of Asian states who do not enjoy a happy history with China will react especially, Japan, India and Vietnam. Under the grand strategy of "off-shore balancing" the chances are that US will take a more detached interest in the Asia-Pacific affairs or as is increasingly evident it will be co-opted by the Chinese. Rather, or begin to identify Asia-Pacific as its legitimate area of interest as Christopher R. Hill, Assistant Secretary for East Asian and Pacific Affairs, argued, "China's success in extending its political influence in the Asia-Pacific region and throughout the developing world, is in my view, a logical evolution, closely tied to its emerging economic clout, and certainly is not a zero-sum game for the United States."[68] The issue could be of trade balance between US and China which off-shore balancers recommend should be a strategic trade, that is, it should account for the trade deficit. This will be difficult to attain as the economic interdependence between US and China cannot be accounted for by the trade deficit only as "but today' bilateral links are much more complex' shaped increasingly by foreign investment and the global strategies of multinationals."[69]

Table 2.2

Region's Defence Expenditure

Regions Military Expenditure in US $ billions

Year	Asia and Oceania (Central Asia, East Asia, Oceania and South Asia)	East Asia
1999	136	101
2000	139	104
2001	147	110
2002	154	116
2003	160	122
2004	169	127
2005	177	133
2006	186	140
2007	196	149
2008	206	157
% Change 1999-2008	52	56

Source: SIPRI Yearbook 2009

Table 2.3

Asia-Pacific Countries Defence Expenditure

(Figures in $ billion)

Countries	1999	2000	2001	2002	2003	2004	2005	2006	2007	2008
China	21.6	23.8	28.5	33.4	36.4	40.6	44.9	52.2	57.9	63.6
India	17.15	17.697	18.3	18.256	18.664	21.660	22.891	23.029	23.535	24.176
Bangladesh	.647	.675	.675	.655	.657	.659	.669	.720	.757	.767
Myanmar	...	...	...	...	...	...	...	...	...	...
Thailand	2.113	1.982	2.063	2.087	2.058	1.962	1.977	2.060	2.569	3.003
Cambodia	.928	.86	.784	.719	.723	.701	.706	.765	.855	...
Indonesia	1.710	2.242	2.367	2.486	3.319	3.653	3.571	3.802	4.131	3.824
Laos	.211	.164	.159	.148	.128	.121	.117	.117	.119	.118
Malaysia	1.847	1.677	2.086	2.370	3.022	2.197	3.120	3.054	3.409	3.479
Brunei	.269	.254	.234	.249	.260	.205	.249	.260	.268	.266
Philippines	.807	.853	.794	.833	.920	.857	.865	.880	1.034	.920
Singapore	4.788	4.631	4.741	4.999	5.048	5.143	5.464	5.670	5.806	5.831
Vietnam	...	...	...	...	.910	.906	.945	1.112	1.274	1.327
North Korea	...	...	...	...	...	...	...	...	...	...

Coun-tries	**1999**	**2000**	**2001**	**2002**	**2003**	**2004**	**2005**	**2006**	**2007**	**2008**
South Korea	15.68-9	16.65-2	17.13-3	17.60-5	18.20-4	19.00-4	20.55-4	21.22-4	22.11-9	23.77-3
Japan	43.48-4	43.80-3	44.27-6	44.27-5	44.81-8	44.47-6	44.16-5	43.66-6	43.46-0	42.75-1
Taiw-an	8.412	7.807	7.965	7.256	7.357	7.923	7.725	7.323	7.791	9.498
Russi-a	14.00-0	19.10-0	21.20-0	23.60-0	25.10-0	26.10-0	28.50-0	31.20	34.80	38.20
Austr-alia	11.05-7	11.02-5	11.46-9	12.01-3	12.33-5	12.82-1	13.29-2	14.11-2	14.89-6	15.32-1
Unite-d States	329.4-16	342.1-67	344.2-97	387.2-97	440.8-06	480.4-44	503.3-53	511.1-71	524.5-91	548.5-31

Source: SIPRI Yearbook 2009

Conclusion

The US "unipolar moment" will inevitably end. But the alarm which earlier this statement used to generate is no more there, in fact a guarded appreciation of China's rise and its tempered role in global affairs. The moot question is how peacefully this "power transition" will take place. It is the Asian continent, which will be most affected by this power transition or in other words will it become a "cockpit of great power conflicts?" China and India because of their antagonistic history and their close relations with USA, will have to indulge in strategic jugglery. China has embarked on a high economic growth and massive military modernisation to achieve great power status. It is working closely with the sole ***superpower to extend its*** sphere of influence in the Asia-Pacific region. Its increasing influence is helped by its high economic growth, which has made it the locomotive of the economic growth in the region. Tide has turned in favour of China. China has refrained from antagonizing the US in a major way. Rather, it has entered into a cooperative relationship with the US in helping especially in the case of rogue states. That is, it is practicing "concessionary balancing." This is inevitable seeing the preponderance of US and China is yet to occupy the other pole.

Endnotes

1 Alan Macmi llan, Ken Booth and R ussell Trood, "Str ategic Cul ture", in Alan Macmillan, Ken Booth and R ussell Trood, *Strategic Cul tures in the Asia-P acific Region* (New Y ork, St. Martin' s Pr ess, 1999), p .8.

2 Yosef Lapid and Friedrich Kr atochwil, eds, *The Return of Cul ture and I dentity in IR Theory* (Boulder, Colo.: Lynne Rienner, 1996).

3 Colin S Gray, " In Praise of Strategy", *Review of International Studies,* Vol. 29, no.2, 2003.

4 Ibid.,

5 Colin S. Gray *Modern Strategy* (Oxford: OUP, 1999)

6 Theodor e de B arry, Twing Tsit Chan and B urton Watson, *Introduction to Oriental Civilizations: Sources of Chinese Tadition* (New York, Columbia University Press, 1960), p .17.

[7] Ibid.

[8]Brian Hook and Denis T witchett eds., *The Cambridge Ency clopaedia of China* (Cambridge, Cambridge University Press, 1991) 2 nd Edition.

[9] John King Fairbank, *China: A New History*, (Cambridge, Massachusetts, London: The Belknap Press, 1992).

[10] Alastair Iain Johnston, *Cultural Realism: Strategic Culture and Grand Strategy in Chinese History* (Princeton: Princeton University Press, 1995), p. 249.

[11] Huiyun Feng, *Chinese Strategic Culture and Foreign Policy Decision Making: Confucianism, Leadership and W ar* (Routledge: London and New Y ork, 2007),pp.25-25.

[12] Ibid. p.26.

[13] Ibid.

[14] Ibid. p.12.

[15] Ibid, p.13.

[16] Rosita Dellios, *Modern Chinese Defence Strategy: Present Development, Future Directions* (Hampshire; Macmillan, 1989), p .27.

[17] Gerald Segal, D *efending China* (Oxford: Oxford University Press, 1985), p.58.

[18] Nan Li, "The PL A's Evolving War fighting Doctrine, Str ategy and T actics, 1985-1995: A Chinese P erspective", David Shambaugh and Richar d H. Y ang, ed., *China's Military in Transition* (Oxford: Clarendon Press, 1997), p .179.

[19] Michael Pllsbury, *China; Debates the Futue Security Environment* (Washington DC: NDU, 2000), p. 273.

[20] Y ou Ji, *The Armed F orces of China* (London, New Y ork: I.B. Tauris, 1999), p.47.

[21] Kevin Pollpeter, "The Chinese Vision of Space Military Operations", James Mulvenon and David Finkelstein, eds., *China's Revolution in Doctrinal Affairs: Emerging Trends in the Operational Art of the Chinese People's Liberation Army* (Alexandria, Virginia: The CNA, 2005), p.368.

[22] Ibid., p.369.

[23] Mark Burles and Abram N. Shulsky, *Patterns in China's Use of Force: Evidence from History and Doctrinal Writings* (Santa Monica, CA: Rand, 2000), p.76.

[24] Ibid., However, even in case of Confucian-Mencian paradigm force can be used, but this can be done only by first exhausting all means of accommodation, resultantly the force used should be minimal and defensive in orientation, until the moral political order is restored.

[25] Joel S. Migdal, Atul Kohli and Vivienne Shue, eds. ,*State Power and Social Forces: Domination and Transformation in the Third World* (Cambridge: Cambridge University Press, 1994).

[26] Vivienne Shue, "State Power and Social Organisation in China", Joel S. Migdal, Atul Kohli and Vivienne Shue, eds. *State Power and Social Forces: Domination and Transformation in the Third World* (Cambridge: Cambridge University Press, 1994), p. 68.

[27] Ibid., p.72.

[28] Ibid., p.73.

[29] Ibid., p.75.

[30] Chinese leaders and strategists are sensitive of discourses, and constraining effects of discourse on their growth. It is because of this that they changed China's rise to peaceful development. The feeling is that US led Western analysts seek to paint China's rise as dangerous. Therefore, they often assert they are only a developing country.

[31] Steve Chan, *China, The US, and the Power-Transition Theory: A Critique* (Routledge: London and New York, 2008), p.94. Chan further argues that in Chinese perspective, "challenges to dominant power are viewed less in terms of contests of raw power and more as an attempt aimed at influencing its incentives and calculations."

[32] http://www.mfa.gov.cn/eng/wjb/zzjg/gjs/gjzzyhy/2612/2614/t15319.htm.

[33] Ibid.,

[34] Cai Peng Hong, 'Non-traditional Security and China and ASEAN Relations: Co-operation, Commitments and Challenges,' in Ho Khai Leong and Samuel C. Y. Ku, (eds.), *China and Southeast Asia: Global Challenges and Regional Challenges* (Singapore: ISEAS, 2005), p.149.

[35] Zhang Yunling and Tang Shiping, "China's National Strategy", in David Shambaugh eds., *Power Shift: China and Asia's New Dynamic* (Los Angeles: University of California Press, 2005), p.49.

[36] Tiejun Zhang, "East Asian Community and China", in Jiemian Yang et al, *Asian Regionalism on the Rise and International System in Transformation* (Shanghai: SIIS, 2007), p.14.

[37] Gerald Segal, "Does China Matter?" Siddharth Mohandas, *The Rise of China* (New York: CFR, 2002).

[38] Chong-pin Lin, " Beijing's New Grand Strategy: An Offensive with Extra-Military Instruments", available at, http://www.jamestown.org/single/?no_cache=1&tx_ttnews%5Btt_news%5D=4006

[39] Avery Goldtsein, "The Diplomatic Face of China's Grand Strategy: A Rising Power's Emerging Choice", *The China Quarterly*, Vol. 168, 2001, p.851.

[40] Michael D. Swaine and Ashley J. Tellis, *Interpreting China's Grand Strategy: Past, Present, and Future* (Rand, Santa Monica, 2000) pp. 97-98.

[41] Christopher La yne, "The Unipolar Il lusion: Why New Gr eat Power Will Rise," *International S ecurity,* Vol.17, No .4 (Spring 1993), pp .551.

[42] Christopher Layne, "The Unipolar Illusion Revisited: The Coming End of the United States' Unipolar Moment", *International Security,* Vol.31, No.2, (Fall 2006), p.8.

[43] Ibid., pp. 8-9.

[44] David Sanders, " I nternational Relations: Neo-Realism and Neo-l iberalism", in Robert E. Goodin and Hans- Dieter Kl ingemaneds., *A New Handbook of P olitical Science* (Oxford, Oxford University Press, 1996). The concessional realism was first used by R D Spengle, "Alarums and Excursions: the state of the discipline in international r elations."*Politickon* (South Af rica), 10, 1983.

[45] P aul Kennedy,*The Rise and F all of Gr eat P owers: Economic Ex change and Military Confl ict from 1500 to 2000* (New Y ork: R andom House, 1987).

[46] Stephanie Kleine- Ahlbrandt and Andrew Sall, "China's New Dictatorship Diplomacy: I s B eijing P arting wi th P ariahs",*Foreign Af fairs,* January/ F ebruary 2008.

[47] http://www.encyclopedia.com/doc/1O999-concession.html.

[48] Evan S. Medeiros, *China's International Behaviour: Activism, Opportunism, and Diversification* (Santa Monica, CA, Rand, 2009), p. xx.

[49] Joseph S. Nye, *Soft Power: The Means to Success in World Politics* (Harvard: Public Affairs, 2004).

[50] David Shambaugh "Return to the Middle Kingdom? China and Asia in the Early Twenty-First Century" Da vid Shambaugh, ed. , *Power Shi ft: China and Asia' s New Dynamics*(Berkeley: University of California Press, 2005), p.23.

[51] Christopher La yne, "China's Chal lenge to US Hegemon y", *Current History*, January 2008, p .17.

[52] Robert S Ross "Engagement in US China Policy" in Alistair Ian Johnston and Robert S Ross, eds. *Engaging China: The Management of an Emergent Power* (London: Routledge, 1999); Michael Oskenberg and Elizabeth Oskenberg , "Introduction: China Joins the World" in Elizabeth Economy and Michael Oksenberg, eds., *China Joins the W orld: Pr ogress and Pr ospects* (New York: Council on Foreign Relations, 1999).

[53] Yuan-Kang Wang "China's Grand Strategy and US Primacy: Is China Balancing American Power" Brookings Institution, http://www.brookings.edu/papers/2006/07china_wang.aspx,p.15.

[54] Dale Copeland, "Economic Interdependence and the Future of US-Chinese Relations" in G John Ikenberry and Michael Mastanduno, eds*International Relations Theory and the Asia-P acific* (New Y ork : Columbia Univ ersity Pr ess, 2003), p . 338.

[55] Ibid.

[56] www.china.org.cn.

[57] G John Ikenberry, "The Rise of China and the Futur e of West: Can the Liberal System Surviv e", *Foreign Affairs,* January/February 2008.

[58] Christopher La yne, "China's Chal lenge to US Hegemon y," *Current History,* January 2008, p . 17.

[59] Ibid., p. 18.

[60] Ibid., p.18.

[61] David Shambaugh, "China Engages Asia: R eshaping the Regional Or der", *International S ecurity,* Vol. 29, No .3, (Winter 2004/2005),p .92.

[62] Yuqun Shao, "The Shanghai Cooper ation Or ganisation and the Dev elopment of Sino-US R elations" in Jiemian Y ang et al, *Asian R egionalism on the Rise and International S ystem in T ransformation* (Shanghai: SIIS, 2007), p .80.

[63] Thomas Lu et al "China's "Soft Power" in Southeast Asia*Congressional Research Service Report for Congress* January 4, 2008, p.10.

[64] Ibid. ,p.19.

[65] Wang Gungwu "China and Southeast Asia: The Context of a New Beginning" in David Shambaugh, ed., *Power Shift: China and Asia's New Dynamics*

(Berkeley: University of California Press, 2005).

[66] Joshua K urlantzick, "China's Charm Of fensive in S outheast Asia," in *Current History,* September 2006, pp .273- 4 .

[67] Ibid. p.276.

[68] Christopher R. Hill, Assistant Secretary for East Asian and Pacific Affairs, "Emergence of China in the Asia-Pacific: Economic and Security Consequences for the U .S." in testimon y bef ore the S enate F oreign R elations Commi ttee, Subcommittee on East Asian and Pacific Affairs.

[69] Joseph P Quinlan, "Ties That B ind", in?" Siddharth Mohandas, *The Rise of China* (New York: CFR, 2002), p .100.

Chapter 3

China and Northeast Asia: Strategic Coexistence

Introduction

It is undeniable that China's most formidable security and foreign policy challenge comes from the North East Asian periphery. North East Asia has been one of the most fragile regions of the world, both during the Cold War and the post-Cold war period. The end of the Cold war has not resulted in mitigating strategic uncertainty. According to Buzan, "the ending of the Cold War had surprisingly little effect on local security affairs in Northeast Asia. Since the indigenous regional issues had largely run in geo-strategic parallel with the Cold War ones, all that was revealed by the removal of the Soviet factor was how important the underlying regional level had been all along."[1] Strategic uncertainty is one of the defining characteristics of the region.

The region is made dangerous by the unpredictable behaviour of North Korea. It exploded nuclear devices twice in the last decade. Its practice of brinkmanship is continuing as evident in the recent sinking of South Korean ship Cheonan. From the Chinese perspective, it can be also said that it is yet to arrive at a *modus vivendi* on strategic relationship in this region. North East Asia as seen in the Track II initiative North East Asia Cooperation Dialogue (NEACD) comprises of China, Russia, United States, two Koreas and Japan. Northeast Asia comprises of critical territory of Taiwan, whose unsettled status from Chinese perspective gives rise to a host of issues. "Northeast Asia conflates in one place all the challenges of the new world order that pivot around two central concerns: the source of possible threats to the regions stability and the feasible and desirable conflict management models to establish peace and prosperity in the region"[2]. Mongolia is also included in the NEA, this chapter doesn't discusses it as it is a minor player in the security affairs of the region.

North East Asia: A Paradox in Region

North East Asia presents a paradox in terms of region. " It is a unique, combustible cocktail of *sui generis* regional characteristics-high capability, abiding animus, deep albeit differentiated entanglement of the Big Four in Korean Affairs, North Korea's recent emergence as "a loose nuclear cannon, the absence of multilateral security institutions, and the resulting uncertainties and unpredictability in the international politics of Northeast Asia"[3] Its constituents are as divergent as world's only superpower United States, the emerging superpower China, world's second largest economy Japan, world's poorest nuclear power North Korea, and South Korea, one half part of state thinking of unification with other half under the threat of nuclear weapons and missiles. Russian representation in the region is made by its Far East territory, which is one of the least developed areas of its territory. Russia aims to play an important role but it's a dependent existence on China. While the region lacks many usual criterion of region (the most important being close economic understanding) it is also least institutionalised. Most importantly it continues with its "expectant" tradition of Cold War, which mulled over the dynamics of triangle between US, USSR and PRC. Now the debate is over emerging equation between PRC and USA, or US, PRC and Japan, and PRC, Japan and South Korea. Further, the issue is of

Japan's normalisation and unification of two Koreas. In game theoretic language it is in dynamic equilibrium.

United States due to its preponderant presence is difficult to categorise as the outsider or insider, even as contradictory pulls and pressures are felt over its presence and rationale in the region. Most importantly US involvement in North East Asia and Chinese refusal to renounce use of force in case of Taiwan asserts independence, risks region to an open ended military duel. Also, United States has guaranteed security to Taiwan in Taiwan Relations Act 1979. In case of Taiwan the puzzle is also over, how the issue will be settled, and what will be the mechanism to arrive at such a settlement. Will the settlement arise of natural process of dialogue and seeming similarities, which have been accentuated by the close economic interdependence. Or its settlement will be a part of power struggle or quid pro quo between the superpower and the rising power.

The other major constituent country of Northeast Asia, Japan represents a challenge not only to Chinese foreign and security policy but also its national identity. China has to manage this relation in order to consolidate its strategic influence in the Asia-Pacific region. Japan represents brutal colonialism, which still raises strong emotions in the Chinese society and politic.[4] Also, Japan is the key ally of United States in the Asia-Pacific, which has stationed near 50,000 forces in the country. Japan not only affects China's regional security and foreign policy, but is also a factor in Sino-US relations. With the recent war of words over between US and Japan over Okinawa base, much seems to be at the centre of duel. And the other critical territory is the Korean Peninsula, with North Korean nuclear brinkmanship region is getting under increasing attention. South Korea with one of the modern developed economies of the region and a key ally of the United States with troops stationed in its territory makes it critical for the Chinese security calculus. The question of unification of two Koreas and their likely foreign policy is a key question. Most importantly, the doubts over implications of China, therefore if any concerted attempts to balance China will take place, its first sign will definitely come up in the North East Asia. Rather, North East Asia will remain the main theatre from which watch on China's Rise will take place.

The question of framework of analysis in which the security dynamics of North East Asia are to be studied, Buzan accepts that East Asia was constituting into "a single RSC during the 1990s, Northeast and Southeast Asia still retained some locally based security dynamics."[5] States act not only as according to their power/ position but also on importance of issues from normative to strategic. Some issues are normative some strategic, and some local and other global, it depends upon how the states mutually make it. It will suffice to note that region by the very virtue of presence of China, US and Japan is capable of affecting international politics globally. As, Chinese take a nuanced understanding of international relations. North East Asia constitutes a region, owing to filling the very criterion of region as defined by Buzan, where patterns of amity and enmity are present, in the said area. Also, the economic interlinkages in terms of interconnection between Russian Far East, China's North East, Japan, Taiwan and two Koreas, make it an economically thriving area. Further, security of many of these areas cannot be discussed without each other. China without Japan or US, Korea without China, and Taiwan without China and US. Further, North East Asia by default constitutes into a region, as the South East Asia constituting into a region cannot be doubted, primarily because of ASEAN. It singularly constitutes into a region, attempts to make an East Asia wide institution is in their beginning stages. Many are ASEAN derivative ones like APT, which are unlikely to shed their ASEAN centrality, attempts of East Asia Community is only at ideational stages.

China aims to advance its strategic interests in the region with larger aims of influence at Asia-Pacific level. China's strategy in the region will also emerge as a result of conveniences and contradictions of US superpower status and the role in the region. Despite the various analyses on US's waning influence, it is the most important variable in the global politics. In the United State's quintessential global gaze, by implication it can afford to be relaxed in its approach to the regional, other than maintaining necessary essential requirements for its superpower status and exercise of influence. This disjuncture also expresses in ideological terms, where China focuses on building an East Asia Community, while US primary interest is in maintaining balance of power through bilateral alliances. It is in this disjuncture between scope for relaxation and maintaining essential presence, China can hope to extend its influence. It is not that it is unilaterally determined by US's conscious choices, but it's also equally determined by pressures of the other powers which seek relative autonomy from the constraining influence of superpower's influence. If we come to see what are the essential requirements of the US presence in the Asia-Pacific, both as a regional presence and as a super power. One thing which gives United States presence an unquestionable basis is that it has presence under Pacific Command. This gives a position of military invincibility in the region, which makes United States a resident power. Generally on the question whether China's increasing influence will make US withdraw from the region, US asserts that it is a resident power. 7th Fleet gives it a forward naval presence. This is also coupled with fact that China is a continental power and US is maritime power. China policy of naval modernisation, which is being presently focussed upon, seeks to earnestly fill in the capability gap. While United States had a dependent existence on bases in Japan, South Korea, or even Taiwan, as is called "an unsinkable aircraft carrier". According to Ross, bipolarity between China and US exists in East

Asia, as geopolitics reinforces these dynamics. Because Chinese and U.S. spheres of influence are geographically distinct and separated by water..."[6] Instead picture is not as stark clear as being argued by Ross, the situation is of competition, with countries having their respective advantages. One thing is clear at least in case of China, that it is not status quoist power.[7] It seeks to advance its power and prestige in North East Asia, while a situation of dominance in mainland South East Asian countries as argued by Ross, may give China a periphery of dominance, but its ultimate arrival can only be announced in the North East Asian region, with some sort of *quid pro quo* with Taiwan, which may or may not lead to outright Taiwan integration, but at minimum announces withdrawal of US from the bilateral equation.

It is not argued that United States is willing to abdicate its superpower status, there're some still factors which US will have to zealously guard. Most importantly, that it will not be willing to be outside institutional imagination of region and larger Asia-Pacific neighbourhood. Though there are contrary opinions as well, which argue that United States gives prime importance to its bilateral alliances to uphold regional balance of power. As Peter Katzenstein argues that United States has traditionally looked towards Europe in terms of multilateral alliance and towards Asia in terms of bilateral alliances.[8] Some analysts have raised the fear which has been consistently been raised in terms of economic regionalism, where James Baker's statement is often cited, that attempts on economic regionalism are geared towards exclusion of United States. But the very fact of an appropriate regional architecture is raised, if it finds fruition then it will necessarily be more than two party membership. Though, it taking place in near future is unlikely. Despite the regions importance due to economic reasons, strategic power will still hold the key.

China and Northeast Asia: Asia's Template

It won't be exaggeration to say that Northeast Asia is Asia's template or specifically Asia-Pacific. If Asia-Pacific is believed to contain 36 states(USPACOM figure) with 54 per cent of the global GDP, these constituents of these regions are most powerful. As they contain four official nuclear powers, with nuclear technology capable Japan. It is also institutionally most deficient, Six Party talks is in its incipient stage, only an ad-hoc mechanism. Of the other two major sub–regions of Asia –Pacific, South East Asia and South Asia, South East Asia with ASEAN is institutionally proactive, but by its very nature of ASEAN way is more prone to tackle softer issues or focus on non-traditional areas. South Asian region is Indo-centric with SAARC as its main regional institution. In these three regional subsets of Asia-Pacific, South Asia stand at distant three, though, India is trying best to shift its foreign policy gravity to South East Asia. While, ASEAN was a product of need for the South East Asian countries to transcend their mutual problems and threat of communism. But externally South East Asian countries have competed for attention with North East Asian countries.[9] North East Asian countries have historically been more geopolitically salient. Attracting or maintaining United States attention in the region has been big challenge to them. Of the many regions South East Asia has been the victim of "Washington's attention deficit disorder"[10] though under the new Obama regime, United States has tried to fill in the void in South East Asia, but it has been content to let it become a backyard of Chinese influence. It is in the South East Asian region that China is supposed to be making most gains. In distinction to South East Asia where China has to take easier steps to mollify the South East Asian neighbours, like a very well developed institutional mechanism of ASEAN. China has acceded to Treaty of Amity and Cooperation, and other declarations on security and South China Sea. In fact, espousing peaceful intentions was easy in case of former. But in case of North East Asia, it is not, consequently, it is a challenging task for China.

As with the challenge, the returns are commensurate, if China manages to hold on to this template which is increasingly becoming China friendly, then it will be easier for China to pursue an unchecked rise at the Asia-Pacific level. Also, it will provide China necessary diplomatic dividend to expand its influence in the global and regional sphere. China recognises that its peaceful rise can be scupper only by challenges coming in North East Asia. This challenge can come in typical inside/outside phenomenon, where Taiwan declares itself to be independent. China in its various policy pronouncements has made it abundantly clear that Taiwan unification is the most important agenda on Chinese elite's minds.

While the tail of Taiwan in Sino-US relations is a key determinant of the bilateral relation, but how the bilateral relations wag this tail is important. It is inevitable for China to seek a policy of strategic coexistence in Northeast Asia, as counter-balancing efforts can come from this region. China cannot match United States militarily at least till the next two decades are concerned. Any premature arms build up can lead to unleashing an arms race. In fact it is the constituent of this region that will affect the Chinese global power ambitions. It is in this context that Chinese grand strategy of peaceful periphery will be tested. This intention to create a peaceful neighbourhood cannot be done by pursuing an isolationist or economic autarchic policy, China will have to engage with the neighbouring countries in order to convey its peaceful intention and prevent any counter balancing forces. Chinese elite have recognised that pursuing an uninterrupted economic growth without diluting key national interests and objectives like Taiwan re-unification, is essential to its rise. Showing military resolve in terms of even ready to go for nuclear brinkmanship is important to convey seriousness of its claim of Taiwan.

In the Northeast Asian diplomatic fora therefore Chinese key policy objective is to make its constituent states become part of its economic diplomacy. Except in case of North Korea all have become important partners in Chinese economic miracle. Though, North Korea is economically dependent on food supplies from China. Especially so with the global economic crisis and China continuing to make a strong recovery. Sino-Japan relations have gained stability, which is unlikely to diminish in the near future.

Northeast Asia is the primary theatre of the geopolitical contest in the larger East Asia or Asia-Pacific. China is apprehensive of US aims and policies in the region, as Shen Qiang, argue "US intention of seeking the leading role in the future geopolitics in East Asia and its overall strategy of seeking hegemony as well."[11] It is as the recent events show especially with the new government in Japan an area where much strategic jostling is taking place. China and Taiwan relations continue to be in a state of indefiniteness. The new government in Taiwan under Ma Ying Jeou have stabilised relations with China, but its domestic popularity is fast receding.[12] China and Japan have an historical legacy, which continues to affect the relation even now, with regular disruptions in bilateral relations over the war memorial. Yet, they have plenty to look forward to, in terms of economic interdependence and strategic coexistence. It is guided by this belief that Japanese new dispensation is looking for less United States dependent relationship or more "equal" relationship. In either ways this will be beneficial for China, hence its adroit diplomacy in the region. Where both Japan and United States are seen as focusing on building good relationship with China. Apart from jostling for strategic alignment and realignment, North Korea presents a nuclear and missile threat to the regional periphery. A close regional diplomacy under the mechanism of Six Party Talks is taking place.

Apart from the strategic importance of the region, the region's salience is also due to the future of the economic potential of the region. Japan is the world's second largest economy, which is likely to be overtaken by China, world's third largest economy in all likelihood in the year 2010. South Korea stands at the world's fourteenth largest economy and Asia's fourth. These triad economies constitute more than three fourths of the regions economy including South East Asia and North East Asia. It is here the future economic gravity is slated to shift. In the recent stress on East Asia Community by Japanese Prime Minister the stress is on China, Japan and South Korea as the central focus of the regional economic grouping. There are varieties of economic regional groupings attempted in the region, China's preference is for an ASEAN Plus Three (China, Japan and South Korea).

Asia is anticipating a regional economic architecture, though there are competing ideas with no firm contours shaping place. The various competing ideas are China's preferred APT, US preference for APEC, and India's preference for ASEAN + 6 on the lines of East Asia Summit membership. In all these institutional contests North East Asia occupies an important place. In fact it will decide the future economic architecture in the region. Especially, in the aftermath of the global economic crisis, when the capacity of the United States and European powers to absorb exports from the developing countries subside. The countries will have to turn to big emerging markets like China, India and Brazil.

It is also notable that in terms of regional energy diplomacy, a new far-reaching development is taking place, with recent opening of the pipeline in far eastern Siberia with the port at Vladivostok.

With regions demand for energy is increasing and their dependence on the Sea Lane of Communication in Indian Ocean, the imperative to reduce this dependence was being felt by many countries of North East Asia. The recent inauguration of the East Siberia Pacific Ocean Pipeline (ESPO). It will deliver oil at the port of Vladivostok, which can be shipped to the countries of North East Asia. This pipeline is being termed as Pacific pipeline, which will reduce Russia's dependence on the European markets.

China and North East Asia: Strategic Coexistence

China from its inception has aimed to address the security dilemma in its North East Asian periphery. This regional periphery has been more unstable after the end of Soviet Union. Despite the rhetorical announcements of its communist leaders, the regional security situation was increasingly against its interests. It had also made China to actively seek security through armed interventions as it did in case of Korean peninsula, Vietnam and Sino-Indian border clash. With the regional periphery of Northeast Asia, with shadowy presence of Russia was always in an unfriendly atmosphere. Chinese accepted that they cannot for long sustain this debilitating feature of dual adversary; hence they had to open up a channel for friendship to the United States. This finally culminated as one of the turning point event of the Cold War. China's outlook towards North East Asia had in an important content of strategic dilemma, where Cold War allies of the United States surrounded it. Even after successfully repulsing US forces to the 38th parallel in the Korean peninsula, they had to work for the security benefits. This could only come by normalising relations with the United States. In pursuit of which China did patiently work for the normalising of bilateral relations.

China's regional diplomacy therefore can be very aptly termed as policy of strategic coexistence. By strategic coexistence, it is argued that China has minimum expectations of the region due to intractable relations among the constituents. That is they can focus only on survival, pro-active only in case of economic diplomacy. This can be very well seen in comparison of Southeast Asia and ASEAN. China's goal especially after opening up of the economy under Deng Xiaoping has geared towards strategic coexistence with neighbouring countries. This is essential to keep the regional periphery peaceful in order to pursue economic modernisation. China is following policy of strategic coexistence in the North East Asian periphery, as it has to balance the competing security interests of the states of the region. It is also noteworthy that the region has pacifist state Japan, but also North Korea which has gained notoriety for its nuclear brinkmanship. The die cast in the region is interesting as the pacifist state of the region Japan is tied in a defence treaty with the only superpower United States. While in case of China is allied with the rogue regime of North Korea, whose international behaviour is increasingly coming under strain. South Korea is also an ally of the United States in the region, whose long-term problem with North Korea is yet to be solved. Long term threat from North Korea's nuclearisation is that it can lead to cascading effect in the region which will affect the regional security situation. The country most likely to be negatively affected is the PRC. Hence it has embarked on a jostling regional diplomacy so as to not worsen the security situation.

This in case of China the regional diplomacy is guided towards preventing worsening of the security situation in the region. This could be in the form of North Korea's nuclearisation leading to Japanese nuclearisation. Or inviting intervention from the United States. This is on the desirability of preventing regional security atmosphere to deteriorate. Further, China's strategic interests in the region are as much fragile as others. The worsening of the regional security atmosphere will lead to arms race in the region, which may result in Japan 'normalising'. Japan's normalisation will bring the rivalry of Sino-Japan into regional diplomacy. It will vitiate the China friendly regional atmosphere, which China has built carefully in the region.

China's Strategy in North East Asia: Five Key Principles

First is in alignment with the well-established Chinese grand strategy of peaceful rise. Though, Odgaard, maintains that Northeast Asia is an exception in Chinese grand strategy.[13] Odgaard argues, "China cannot respond by promoting its global grand strategy because the challenges to Chinese security posed by US alliance system in this region are sufficiently grave that China focuses on its survival rather than on increasing its political leverage."[14] Rather, Chinese policies in North East Asia are a continuation of its grand strategy, and going by the regional developments. China is in advantageous position. The variations are only to the extent of adapting it to the regions specificities and constraints. China is aware of the economic potential of the North East Asia. Therefore, the goal is that it has to ensure that its regional policy of peaceful neighbourhood is not compromised. Any alteration in regional balance of power or any armed disturbance is likely to worsen the security situation, and force China to take sides. Rather, China will prefer that its regional periphery is economically thriving in which can also actively contribute. The data for regional economic engagement among the North East Asia countries is a prime example of this strategy. Apart from the economic reason of mutual trade, there is also strategic content as well. Most importantly, increasing economic interdependence will not only change the regional atmosphere but will also pave for shifting of geopolitical priorities. Japan and United States which are the closest allies in this region, will have to alter with the shifting geo-political priorities. In fact, as the People's Republic of China emerges as the world's second largest economy in 2010, by displacing Japan, the economic attention, which is already focussed on China, will become more focussed on it. In the present global economic crisis, China's growth has led to much of the development, especially in last decade where China has averaged nearly 11 % growth rate, Japan has managed only 1.4 %. Increasingly, as Japan prepares to lose second place to China, economic gravity will shift more to China.

The second cardinal principle of Chinese strategy in the region is that ensuring no balancing efforts take place. Chinese policy of peaceful development and rise has to be tested in this regional periphery. It is to the credit of Chinese diplomacy that balancing efforts are not taking place. However, one cannot ignore the fact that the region is still witnessing high rates of military spending.[15] There is variety of reason for this, but China has managed this periphery very well. Even when it has refused to give up its claims on the disputed territories of Taiwan and contested island of Senkaku in East China Sea. At times, bilateral relations and regional security atmosphere was vitiated on competitive claims. It is one of the rarest episodes of international diplomacy where a rising state has refused to give up its claims but has managed to cool the regional atmosphere. Many events have taken up in the region like worsening of the bilateral relations between China and Japan in 2005 over history books. And, over the territory in East China Sea. Though China and Japan have reached a deal over the joint development of gas field in the East China Sea resolving a four-year-old –dispute.

The strategy of China in this region is of no independence to Taiwan or one China policy. In pursuit of this strategy all political, diplomatic and military efforts are to be used to pursue this goal. China's external diplomatic engagement has this condition, of countries recognising one China principle. China has been successful in this. Further, China applied political and military pressure domestically on Taiwan to check its independence ambitions. In the earlier regime of Lee Teng Hua, China and Taiwan were increasingly at loggerheads, with China applying military pressure. To prevent Taiwan's independence China has military overwhelmed the island state, with nearly 150 missiles pointing to the island. Most importantly, China's military preparedness is geared towards access denial strategy in case of conflict breaks out. Further, China asserts their resolve on declaration of not renouncing use of force in case of Taiwan.

Military modernisation is another essential component of China's North East Asia strategy. It is obvious that Chinese great power potential cannot be realised without having a modern and capable military. China's predominant aim is to be major military power in the Asia-Pacific. In order to project power, China has to have blue water navy. Though, Chinese security interests are wide ranging across its boundary. But its military power projection is more aimed in the North East Asian hemisphere. China's military modernisation is aimed at countering United States forces, especially in the contingency of the Taiwan declaring independence.

Finally, a stable Sino-US relation is essential to Chinese strategy in the region. In fact it provides stability in the regional setting for all powers to mutually interact. A good and stable Sino- US relation is essential for larger Chinese grand strategy to come to fruition. Further, United States active involvement in the region has security benefits for the other countries, which can interact with China. This has been one of the avowed policies of the Chinese government. Therefore, instead of pushing for American withdrawal in the North East Asia or Asia-Pacific, as it did in case of calling for American withdrawal from Central Asia in Shanghai Cooperation Organisation. China welcomes United States role and presence in Asia-Pacific. But even in Chinese engagement of United States there is a strategy as well. While China is willing to negotiate its relations with the United States bilaterally, it is hesitant in entering into a multilateral engagement with it especially in the regional context. This explains why China is more interested in Asean Plus Three. It also does not want United States to be part of East Asia Summit. China is aware of that United States presence in a multilateral forum with a regional focus will try to stymie its regional diplomacy. Further smaller neighbours are more likely to try to balance against China. Sino-US relations in a bilateral mode part form the benefits of the bilateral relation also enhances Chinese status in the regional periphery. Further, it restricts the ambit of talks to mutual issues where China can also play the aggrieved party and seek concessions. As, China has gone on amassing power, its need for concessions has declined. But till its accession to WTO (World Trade Organisation) in 2001, China has concessions to seek. But now China has become the party with benefits to offer, now Sino-US relations have become the duel for power and status signalling. It is essential for China that this is the most important bilateral relation, and it is handled very carefully to send right signals to the regional countries. On the one hand, it is essential for China that this relation does not deteriorate so that balancing efforts take place. Also, it does not become too close to be seen as a camp follower of the United States. In this the characteristic Chinese ambivalence is helpful. China has managed at the same time a stable relations with the United States, as well position itself as an alternative pole to it.

China recognises this is the most important bilateral relation, its rise depends upon having a good relation with it. United States five allies will take their cue from US policy in the region. In last five six years US policies towards China has been over all benevolent. The dilemma over US presence in Asia- Pacific has been effectively resolved in favour of US's presence it prevents Japan's breaking out as a "normal" country. Good Sino-US relations are the best regional template of benign China. China has very exploited this changing sentiment in the region. In the recent US President's visit to China, the Chinese were able to turn it into their diplomatic victory.

China and Northeast Asia: Economic Interdependence as the Trump

China, Japan and South Korea increasingly constitute a group of countries whose economic convergence is deepening in the sub-region. Among three they constitute 90 per cent of the East Asian economy and 17 percent of the world economy.[16] This is one of the most dynamic economic regions of the world. It is also playing a more active role in the ASEAN Plus Three mechanism. The three countries have set up a trilateral in 1999 with economic cooperation as the prime focus. This has contributed to trade among them growing from $130 billion to $500 billion[17]. The aim of the three countries has been to embed this trilateral in the larger regional focus of East Asia under APT. Among them they constitute 70 per cent of the Asia's GDP. This has been the prime aim of the Chinese sub-regional policy before it thinks of any strategic preponderance; its aim is to make the region economically interdependent.

In this it has been quite successful; China has become Japan's number one trade partner. South Korea has embarked on a high growth trade pattern, Taiwan's economy has become so much dependent on the Chinese economic growth that voices are being raised over the strategic consequences of this one sided dependence. Russia has also begun to take part in the regions economic success, especially with the opening of the new Eastern Siberia Pipeline. It will reduce much of the energy insecurity in the region.

China, Japan and South Korea have set-up a Trilateral in 1999, which once again reflected Chinese desire to engage in multilateral diplomacy in an economic forum. Recently, the trilateral has celebrated its tenth anniversary with a meeting of the trilateral in October 2009 in Beijing, China. The Joint Statement emphasised on:-

> The three countries remained committed to the development of an East Asia community based on the principles of openness, transparency, inclusiveness as a long-term goal, and to regional cooperation, while maintaining increased trilateral communication and coordination on regional and international affairs.[18]

The trilateral composed of three countries, is planning of establishing a Secretariat. But their vision is far from being sub-regional; rather focus on the formation of East Asia community. The tug of war is especially over what shape it takes place. These three countries are key to the financial institutional imagining of the East Asia. In fact it is to the credit of the Chinese and Japanese cooperation that East Asia wide financial structure in the form of Chiang Mai initiative is taking place.[19] Even though Japan is careful that it does not plays into Chinese hands by backing any financial structure which may be anathema to the United States. China which has gained much brownie point in the Asian financial crisis aims to solidify in the form of Chang Mai initiative. While initially the formation of Asian Bond Market Initiative under the Japanese leadership could not fructify because of US opposition and Chinese reluctance to support the Japanese initiative for the fear it taking leadership position in the region.

China subsequently changed its position and was more than willing to work with Japan on promoting the Chiang Mai Initiative. US has also become less suspicious of the Chiang Mai initiative taking the form of Asian Monetary Fund. This has also to do with the origin of the initiative itself. It took its origin in ASEAN stable of institutions though later picked by both China and Japan. China has supported in its larger foreign policy aims and objectives, where its aim is to use its economic power as the attraction to increase its influence in the region. China does not want to challenge US military in the region. But tries to use economic influence and economic market as the means to reduce US influence in the region. This is one of the fears being raised over the trade competition in the Asia-Pacific. American insistence is over the Trans Pacific Partnership. Though, China is also part of the APEC, it is more interested in the advancing economic integration in the regional APT mechanism than APEC.

While the United States has a Strategic and Economic Dialogue with China, now even Secretary of State is also present in the meetings. But here the Chinese strategy is have the Sino-US relations at the global plane and bilateral level. US Asian diplomacy is focused on five alliances. But the issue remains as the Chinese regional economic profile changes it will be especially difficult to say how the regional allies cope with it. Presently, states are actively participating in the economic opportunities offered by China especially in the global economic crisis. But the dilemmas of Chinese economic growth poses are beginning to show especially in the Japanese foreign policy. The new government of Yukoi Hatoyama expressing a desire for a more equal relationship with the United States. This especially becomes all the more pressing when China becomes one of the top most economic partners. The dilemma of continuing strong relationship with the United States as it is under its nuclear deterrence that Japan is reaching security benefits. But it has also to see that the economic future is tied up with Chinese economic fortunes. China is strategically astute not to push its strategic interests.

Energy security of the region is likely to create much of geopolitical problems in the North East Asia. According to Kent E. Calder, the growing energy needs in North East Asia will amplify geopolitical rivalries.[20] This is especially true for Japan, which imports 90 per cent of its oil requirements. Japan dependence on oil resources of middle East and consequently on Sea Lanes of Communication is leading to energy angst. Russia's opening of the Eastern Siberia Pacific Ocean Pipeline is likely to engender new energy diplomacy in the region.

China-Japan

Sino-Japan relations are key determining factors in the sub-region, but it will have larger systemic importance. The factors affecting the relationship are the historical factors and future events. In case of Sino-Japan relations much is at stake but at the same time they carry a historical baggage. In case, of China a feeling of victim and Japan as the aggressor. While at the same time the relation is of anticipation, while China is likely to displace Japan as the number one economic power in Asia-Pacific, and on the other hand Japan's 'normalisation' is still a matter of debate.

China has still problems over colonial history of Japan, which many Japanese analysts see it as an attempt by China to check its regional role. China's national identity is entwined with the Japanese colonialism and sense of victimhood. According to the recent Pew Global Attitudes Report, only 11 percent of the population has a favourable view of Japan and regard it as partner, 38 per cent regard it as enemy and 38 per cent are indifferent.[21] While at the same time domestic opinions on either side accuse each other of being more stridently nationalist.[22]

Japanese have forfeited their normal military status in the Second World War and adopted a Peace constitution under Article 9, which forbids normal military. With the United States presence under the Mutual Defence treaty, Japan is under the nuclear umbrella of United States.[23] China's natural security interests are against Japan taking a normal military posture.[24]

It will worsen its security interests in the neighbourhood. Coupled with the US presence it will lead to balancing tendency in the region. China's policy here is to make region peaceful, so that it can pursue its economic growth. Therefore, it will like that the relations between China and Japan are as mutually beneficial as possible. Increasing economic interdependence, which both the countries are pursuing, can do this. China is willing to concede economic space and work jointly with Japan. In Japan opinions are also being voiced over the need for realignment with the new situation in the Northeast Asia, especially China's new position of influence as Tanaka said, "Japan must restructure its foreign policy to better suit its new environment. In recent years, Japanese foreign policy has been plagued by overdependence on the United States, insufficient attention to China's emergence as a challenger for regional leadership..."[25]. Former Deputy Foreign Affairs Minister, delineate five points for the re-orientation of Japan's Asia policy. It involved,

(1) achieving a "grand bargain" with China;

(2) institutionalizing a trilateral security dialogue among Japan, China, and the United States;

(3) maintaining the Six-Party Talks as a mechanism for subregional consultations on security issues;

(4) establishing an East Asia Security Forum; and 5) creating a region wide rules-based economic community.[26]

The pressures on Japan to adapt to the changing East Asian strategic landscape is immense, but the means of this adjustment are limited, and almost all the means have to give prime importance to China. It will not be overstatement to say that, Japan is in quandary over appropriate policy towards China, therefore various formulations express this dilemma. Some author's call it as a "façade of friendship".[27] Self argues that "China and Japan are balanced on a razor's edge between closer cooperation and dangerous rivalry."[28] If it is a "grand bargain", on many lingering issues of history, and reconciliation takes place. It has to discredit the China threat theory, and has to move closer to China in terms of bilateral relations. Or as Tanaka points out, emphasis on trilateral of USA, China and Japan, takes place, it will essentially mean that China has been accounted with its new geopolitical status and weight. Forging an East Asia Community, as the recent Prime Ministers stressed on is likely to be seen as giving into Chinese long term plans of forging an East Asia Community and falling into a well thought out Chinese strategy. As, the recent economic recovery in Japan from recession is in part derived from the Chinese economic growth. But in long term there are "fears that Japan will find itself relegated to its premodern era status as a subordinate power in East Asia."[29] China and Japan are also competing over signing of Free Trade Area with Asean countries, former has taken a lead much to resentment of Japan. Japan has begun to change its orientation to the ASEAN with the Hashimoto Doctrine in 1997, this has catapulted the relation to the new level, helping in the institutionalisation of summit meetings through ASEAN + 3 venues, but "it is China that is reacting to the fast changing regional environment, not Japan."[30]

China's emergence as the pre-eminent economic power and military power is likely to pose an identity problem to Japan. The easiest recourse will be to strengthen Japan-US alliance, after much discussion and debate as the recent signing commemorating 50 years of Japan-US Defence Treaty, which enjoins, "the United States and Japan will continue to deepen their cooperation, including that between U.S. forces and Japan's Self Defense Forces, in wide-ranging areas of common interest in the changing security environment."[31] But in the long term the alliance will "10 or 15 years from now the US-Japan alliance may no longer be able to provide a sufficient hedge against the military capabilities of China."[32] Further, Taiwan is also an irritation in the bilateral alliance, where Japan has openly expressed its support for the use of US bases in its territory for Taiwan's defence. Japan will face two stark choices, either it has to normalise with the full status of normal military power or push for a multilateral forum, it is doubtful whether forging multilateral frameworks without fully normalising is fruitful. While China's stress on having a good relations with Japan is critical for technological flows, especially in the energy and technological cooperation. According to Tsunekawa Jun, "energy security cooperation is one of the areas in which Japan contributes to China's development and environmental protection, as mentioned above, through providing energy –saving technologies."[33] This is likely to be a solace but as a mark of future oriented strategy, but it is also likely to cause a heart burn, as China will use Japanese technology and FDI to achieve an unassailable position in North East Asia. This will be an example of cold politics and hot economics. According to Kang Japan is likely to follow a policy of omnienmseshmnet or omnidirectional foreign policy for the time being[34], whether it will lead to dampening of security anxieties is difficult to say.

In short, the China-Japan relationship will maintain continue with incremental progress, with pangs of doubt plaguing Japanese decision makers. Japanese will worry about the increasing influence of China, with their interest more in East Asia than in its global ambitions. Though the logical step will be to normalize and Asianise, but it will involve lots of geopolitical courage to do so. Seeing the difficulty in Yukio Hatoyama's attempt to shift Okinawa base, it is likely that Japan will continue with the present trend hoping to maintain its economic salience and follow a policy of gradual regional enmeshment.

China-Taiwan

Taiwan represents China's many intractable inside/outside difficulties. The most important are of nation building and identity, the renegade province of Taiwan is representative of the unfulfilled task of the twentieth century. Now with United Sates occupying a permanent presence in its security calculus, it is symbolic of an external actor present in China's internal affairs. China's principal region of influence is Asia-Pacific, where it has embarked on an extensive diplomacy to improve its ties. The core security concern of China remains the Taiwan issue. It is to the credit of Chinese diplomacy that it has managed to ensure that status quo is not violated. Mainland China and Taiwan have managed to establish a vibrant trade relationship between them coupled with this is that US the main supporter of Taiwan also adheres to the One China policy it does provide military arms and ammunition to bolster the defence of Taiwan. But the purpose is only to ensure that China does not takeover Taiwan forcefully. China has refused to renounce the use of force in the context of Taiwan proceeding from *de facto* independence to *de jure* independence. This situation of stalemate is likely to continue but with change that China in the future will able to seek some concessions from the US on the Taiwan. US traditional policy on Taiwan has been that "cross-strait relations must be resolved peacefully." Though, the advocates of off-share balance strategy argue "a possible showdown between China and Taiwan simply would not justify the risks and costs of US intervention." In this circumstance, both the states have limited option other than to continue with the stalemate. However, it is for sure that US will counsel restraint to both the parties. But the bottom line will be that US will be increasingly unwilling to risk men and material for Taiwanese independence rather coerce and cajole it to seek some sort of via-media with the mainland China. As Campbell and Mitchell argue "for past two decades the essence of US policy in the Taiwan Strait has been to preserve peace and stability in the region while indefinitely deferring the ultimate resolution of the problem."[35]

Major General Xiong Guankai, former Director General of Military Intelligence said that in case of show of force over Taiwan, United States will value Los Angeles more than Taiwan. It was one of the most cited statements showing bellicosity of Chinese political and military class. With United States guaranteeing security of the state Chinese elite have to consider military contingency operations. China has refused to allow full statehood to the Taiwan. While earlier China has used muscle flexing to keep the nations activity in check. But in the present dispensation of Ma Ying Jeou, the relations have cooled. China is seeking maintenance of "status-quo". Yet the long-term military preparation of area denial and anti-access strategies is being pursued. On the other hand between China and Taiwan direct flights have started and trade has taken up in a big way. It is also to be noted that people to people relations have grown. In case of Taiwan all three parties have an interest in status quo, but it is not difficult to say which party is likely to make more relative gains. It is undoubtedly China whose economic growth has led to accretions in Chinese military power. While United States is present in cross-straits relations emphatically denying any resort to force and giving arms to Taiwan. It has to in the long term give recognition to China's new status as the Asia-Pacific power.

Korean Peninsula

China's goal of strategic coexistence has manifested in the case of the North Korea as well. China in deference to the international public opinion actively used its leverage over North Korea to defuse the tension in the Korean peninsula. It acted as a crucial mediator in the region. China has been playing crucial role in ensuring that the North Korea comes to the negotiating table. Chinese role has been critical as can be discerned from the fact that before the major events of Three Party Talks (April 2003) and Six Party Talks First Round (August 2003) and Second Round (December 2003). Chinese delegation visited Pyongyang.[36] China and North Korea, which have traditionally patron-client relationship, did not stop it from unequivocally condemning July 4, 2006 missile test by North Korea. However, China opposed the sanctions on it. On October 2, 2006, when North Korea tested nuclear weapons. China was quick to denounce it as brazen and it said "firmly opposing the nuclear test and strongly demanding that North Korea should keep its promise to be a non-nuclear weapon state." It voted in favour of the Security Council Resolution 1718 condemning its nuclear test. North Korea is yet to agree to full de-nuclearisation, and has put the condition of a peace Treaty with United States, before it gives up its nuclear weapons and ballistic missiles.[37] US has refused to enter into any deal before denuclearisation of the Korean peninsula takes place.

Conclusion

China's policy in North East Asia, cannot be anything but of strategic coexistence amply helped through burgeoning economic linkages. While the former is recognition of the seeming intractability of strategic relationship latter is recognition of economic globalisation. The region due to its high geopolitical anxiety, with China, US, Russia, and North Korea (all nuclear powers) can only aim for a minimum geopolitical coexistence. Any ambitious policy of restructuring region is bound to fail and may be counter-productive. Setting up of Six Party talks against North Korean nuclearisation exemplifies the inherent instability of the region, where six countries have to come together to deal with it. This instability has been experienced before even during the initial years of the Cold War. China is prudently following the policy of economic engagement, which subserves its larger grand strategy of economic growth. Further it also contributes in progress of Six Party talks. Chinese strategy in the region is best achieved in terms of preventing region from deterioration in security, rather favours configuring region in economic terms. The region is likely to continue with this anomalous situation with high economic interdependence but low on geopolitical trust. This anomalous situation is likely to produce its own stresses and strains. While China, Japan and South Korea are increasingly focusing on trilateral as a means of realising East Asia Community. What shape it will take place only time can tell. While simultaneously support is also there for trilateral composing of China Japan and United States. But North East Asia will continue to in state of unpredictability till a strategic realignment takes place. But for this realignment to take place it will be essential for Japan to accept a second status to China and United States willing to concede North East Asia as under China's legitimate sphere of influence. This is unlikely to take place at least in the near future. China's desire to extend its influence to Asia-pacific in mirror image to its traditional middle kingdom complex will force it to make military preparations. Further the regions' simultaneous capacity of action regionally and globally will raise an entire gamut of issues, which have keen stressed by power transition theories.

The region is locked up in a series of strategic equations, which are difficult to unravel without upsetting the traditional stabilizing factors. Like China's regional aspiration will continue to rise, as it gains more economic progress far more sinister is the development that China's military is locked up in security dilemma over Taiwan with the United States. Thus pressure on China to advance it naval capacity is very much there. Also, with China's advance Japan will increasingly feel pressure and the need to align its foreign policy to Asia, as its focus has been long extra-regional. But will this resetting of focus will come up with traditional Japanese policy of pacifism, or Japan will alter its defence policy as well. It is unlikely that Japan will like to reduced to a second power in the region. Rather it will more rely on United States to gives its exceptional status in the international politics. Though, internally there is opposition over military bases but it is likely that despite disaffection the facilities will continue. Most importantly the unpredictable issue is over the Korean peninsula the brinkmanship of North Korea and issue of unification.

Endnotes

[1] Barry Buzan and Ole W eaver, *Regions and P owers: The Structure of International Security* (Cambridge, Cambridge University Press, 2003), p.152.

[2] Samuel S. Kim, "Northeast Asia in the Local-Regional-Global Nexus: Multiple Challenges and Contending Explanations", Samuel S. Kim, *International Relations of Northeast Asia.* (Lanham, Rowman & Littlefield Publishers, 2004), p.9.

[3] Ibid., p.9.

[4] In the year 2005, Sino- Japan relations deteriorated over the Japanese textbooks, which China claimed glossed over its World War II atrocities. The protests in many places in China took a violent turn.

[5] Barry Buzan and Ole Weaver,*Regions and Powers: The Structure of International Security*, p. 152.

[6] Robert S. Ross, "The Geography of the Peace: East Asia in the Twenty First Century",*International Security*, 23, 4 , 1999, p .99.

[7] Alastair Iain Johnston," Is China a Status Quo Power ?" , *International Security,* Vol 27, No.4 (Spring 2003).

[8] Peter J. Katzenstein, *A World of Regions: Asia and Europe in the American Imperium* (Ithaca, NY: Cornell University Press, 2005).

[9] Alice D. Ba, *Re[Negotiating] East and South East Asia: Region, Regionalism and ASEAN* (Stanford University Press, 2009).

[10] Alice Ba, "Systemic Neglect? A Reconsideration of US-Southeast Asia Policy", *Contemporary South East Asia,* Vol. 31, No . 3, 2009 .

[11] Shen Qiang, "Pluralistic Geopolitics in East Asia: Evolving in Ups and Downs", *International Strategic Studies,* 4th June 2007 .

[12] John Pomfret and Blaine Harder, "Wary Japan redefines relationship with US", *The Washington Post,* 22 October 2009.

[13] Liselotte Odgaard, "Chinese Northeast Asia policies and the tragedy of Northeast Asia's Security Architecture", *Global Change, Peace & Security,* Vol.20, No.2, June 2008.

[14] Ibid. , p.190.

[15] John Feffer, "An Arms Race in Northeast Asia?" *Asian Perspective,* Vol.33, No. 4, 2009. Also see, Zhu Feng, "An Emerging Trend in East Asia: Military Budget Increases and their Impact", *Asian Perspective,* Vol. 33, No . 4, 2009.

[16] Remarks by Premier Wen Jiabao At the First China-Japan-ROK Business Summit available at http://www .fmprc.gov.cn/eng/wjdt/zyjh/t623025.htm.

[17] Ibid.

[18] http://www .mofa.go.jp/region/asia-paci/jck/meet0910/joint-1.pdf.

[19] Hyoung-kyu Chey, "The Changing P olitical Dynamics of East Asian Financial Cooperation: The Chiang Mai I nitiative, *Asian Survey,* Vol. 49, I ssue 3, 2009.

[20] Kent E. Calder, "*Japan's* Energy Angst and Caspian Great Game", *NBR Analysis,* Vol 12, No ,1, Mar ch 2001.

[21] *The 2008 Pew Global Attitudes Survey in China:* The Chinese Celebrate Their Roaring Economy, As they Struggle with Its Costs near Universal Optimism about Beijing Olympics p.21. July 22, 2008, available at http://pewglobal.org/ 2008/07/22/the-chinese-celebrate-their-roaring-economy-as-they-struggle-with-its-costs/.

[22] Jian Y ang, "Of inter est and distrust: Understanding China' s P olicy Towards Japan", *China: An I nternational Journal,* 5, 2 (S ep.2007), pp .267-272. Y ang argues that, "Nationalism in China is rising, partly because a rapidly growing economy gives the Chinese much pride and confidence and partly because nationalism has been a usef ul rallying tool f or the Go vernment.", p.270.

[23] " 60 % of DPJ lower house members Japan want out of US nuclear Umbrella", *Japan Today,* 11th October, 2009. a vailable at ht tp://www.japantoday.com/ category/politics/view/60-of-dpj-lower-house-members-want-japan-out-of-us-nuclear-umbrella.

[24] "Go vernment to postpone adoption of new def ence out line to next y ear", *Japan Today*, 11 October 2009, a vailable at ht tp://www.japantoday.com/ category/politics/view/govt-to-postpone-adoption-of-new-defense-outline-to-next-year.

[25] Hitoshi Tanaka, "Defining Normalcy: The Future Course of Japan's Foreign Policy", *East Asia Insights: Toward Community Building,* Vol.3, No. 1, January 2008, p.2.

[26] Ibid. p.3.

[27] Benjamin Self, "China and Japan: A Façade of Friendship", *The Washington Quarterly*, 26, 1, Winter 2002-03,

[28] Ibid., p.77

[29] Hitoshi Tanaka, "A Japanese Perspective on China", *East Asia Insights: Toward Community Building,* Vol. 3, No. 2, 2008, p. 2.

[30] Sueo Sudo, "Japan's ASEAN Policy: Reactive or Proactive in the Face of a Rising China in East Asia", *Asian Perspective*, Vol 33, No.1, 2009, p 156.

[31]"Joint Statement of the U.S.-Japan Security Consultative Committee Marking the 50th Anniversary of the Signing of The U.S.-Japan Treaty of Mutual Cooperation and Security", January 19, 2010, available athttp://www.mofa.go.jp/region/n-america/us/security/joint1001.html.

[32] Hitoshi Tanaka, " A Japanese Perspective on China", p.4.

[33] Tsunekawa Jun, "Toward a Stable Relationship between Japan and China: From a Bilateral to Multilateral Approach", Masafumi Iida ed., *China's Shift: Global Strategy of the Rising Power* (Tokyo, NIDS, 2009), p.124.

[34] David C. Kang, *China Rising: Peace, Power, and Order in East Asia* (Sussex, Columbia University Press, 2007).

[35] Kurt Campbell and Derek J Mitchell "Crisis in the Taiwan Strait?" in Siddharth Mohandas ed., *The Rise of China* (New York: Council on Foreign Relations Book 2002), p.55.

[36]Jae Ho Hung, "China's Ascendancy and the Korean Peninsula: From Interest Re-evaluation to Strategic Realignment? in David Shambaugh, ed., *Power Shift:*

China and Asia's New Dynamics (Berkeley: University of California Press 2005), p. 57.

[37] " North K orea Talks For Peace Treaty Talks wi th US ", *International Herald Tribune,* 11 January 2010 , a vailable at ht tp://www. nytimes. com /2010/01/ 12/world/asia12korea.html?scp=1&sq=north%20%20korea%20steephen %20bosworth&st=cse.

Chapter 4

China and South East Asia: Strategic Convergence

Introduction

The benchmark by which China's strategy in the region can be understood, is its grand strategy, as already discussed in Chapter Two. China's overall aim is to emerge as a preponderant power in the Asia-Pacific. The achievement of this objective is a long term plan, but locally necessary conditions should be maintained so as to be conducive to its achievement. Therefore, one of the dominant objectives is that, China's periphery should be peaceful and facilitate its rise. While at the same time it is quite obvious, that international isolation cannot go hand in hand with economic opening. Therefore, China was, convinced that it has to open up strategically as a logical conclusion of economic opening up. China and Southeast Asia relations which have been earlier held hostage to a variety of factors, like support for Communists, intervention in Vietnam, and great power politics. Now, with the end of the Cold war, these tactics may no longer be relevant, rather the gaze is set high on the objective of emerging as a great power. In order to emerge as a great power, China will have to start acting like one. Therefore, China's South East Asia policy is geared towards this end. While the long term objective of emerging as a great power is the key determinant of Chinese behaviour in the region. China looks towards the region for precisely, two reasons, one the growing economic convergence and participating in the multilateral mechanisms of the region, however, tempered, adhoc and incomplete it may be. While the economic convergence has a self–sustaining logic, more important is Chinese approval for multilateral mechanism of the region, or as popularly termed as China's socialisation into multilateralism.

This is a far-reaching transformation in global geopolitics and Chinese diplomacy, which is taking place in this region. This is coupled with and in response to China's rise. It is generally argued that China has acquired an advantageous position in the Southeast Asian region. It can be undoubtedly said that China is taking the lead in the regional politics, but it cannot be denied at the same time, ASEAN has always looked to invite foreign players to enhance its multilateral salience. The preferred external actors could be India, China, Japan or the United States. While, India has consistently pushed for more important role in the regional politics, China has embarked on aggressive diplomacy to counter feelings of suspicion, at the same time United States has been 'off' and 'on' in its attention to South East Asia. United States inconsistent diplomacy has given an opportunity to China to expand its influence in the region. This inconsistent diplomacy may not be altogether new but have a historical basis or pattern. Japan is also trying to match up to Chinese influence in the region. Further, circumstances have developed fortuitously to advance China's influence in the region. The disappearing of USSR, removed one of the challengers and its prop Vietnam to play a competitors role. In China's grand strategy of peaceful development and harmonious existence, Southeast Asia plays an important role. If the Northeast Asian region was not amenable to Chinese influence due to the presence of two big powers Japan and United States, whose interests are in conflict with it. But in Southeast Asia there is no such big power, and United States presence is limited and variegated. Thus, in Southeast Asia, China finds it relatively easy to spread its influence. One of the distinguishing factors of China and Southeast Asian countries relationship is that generally they are not in competition for power or dominance. Individually they are small countries in comparison to China. The biggest country of the region Indonesia stands at the world's 16th position in terms of area, while China stands at number 4.[1] However, apprehension of China's rise is affecting Southeast Asian countries. For China goal is more of reducing this suspicion partly arising out of history partly out of emerging balance of power. But history of China and Southeast Asian countries has not been only negative; they have mutually co-existed in Sino-centric region with relations of hierarchy or tribute. Among China and Southeast Asia relations therefore the challenge is of reducing burdens of history, but using positive factors of cultural links in forming people centric relationship or community; while economically relationship holds significance and potential; and geopolitically arriving at a peaceful co-existence under a multilateral framework is the key. In pursuit of these objectives ASEAN and its derivative institutions can play a very important role.

Further, Southeast Asia has an important role in influencing geopolitics of larger Asia-Pacific. The changing geopolitical equations between the countries of United States, China, Japan and India are likely to be orchestrated in this region. The role of ASEAN becomes crucial in managing the rivalry and pushing the issues from divisive ones to future oriented. The ASEAN and its famous "ASEAN Way" is likely to temper the geopolitical rivalry and tailor it to new channels. Though, ASEAN wouldn't like to be caught between the rivalry of the big powers, and would prefer omni-enmeshment of the powers, which is likely to lead to the benefit of regional co-operation. ASEAN's role here become critical in tempering the geopolitical competition and yet become central to the regional cooperation efforts and exploit the economic advantages coming its way in the rapid pace of economic growth. But the puzzle in the Southeast Asian geopolitics will be whether ASEAN's famed "ASEAN way" is able to keep up with regional geopolitics or itself gets divided over the economic benefits and particular strategic priorirties, and allies with the dominant economic power. In the later case most likely candidate will be China. Instances are being cited when regional countries showed their preference for China. Like in the case of Thailand when in mid-1990s it refused "a request from Washington to station munitions on ships in the Gulf of Thailand."[2] Subsequently, Thailand became a member of Non-Aligned Movement and dithered in responding to United States help in post-September 9/11.

China and Southeast Asia: From Troubled History to Prosperous Present

In the ancient period China and Southeast Asia were linked in Sinocentric world order. The relations from Chinese perspective were of superiority and inferiority, where Southeast Asian states owed tribute to the Chinese kings. While the exact meaning and significance of tribute was not clear, Wang Gungwu argues that "there was never any attempt to be precise about what tributary status meant, and the Chinese were probably wise to leave the question vague and frontiers flexible."[3] He attributes this to the Chinese acute sense of history, by which they want to leave a legacy. While Chinese rulers exacted tributary as a means of superior status and imperial power, the tribute givers had only prudent motive of able to carry on trade. "What for the Chinese was ritual submission to the Son of Heaven was for Southeast Asian rulers a ritual of polite diplomacy required as a condition of trade."[4] It must also be noted that though in contemporary Southeast Asia Chinese cultural influence by way of ancient linkage and ethnic migration is there, but except Vietnam, the Southeast Asian states didn't derived their civilization from China, in fact Hindu and Buddhist ideas formed basis of their civilisation. According to Fairbank, "the other lands of

Southeast Asia beyond Vietnam were never absorbed into the East Asian cultural sphere, but derived much of their civilization from Hindu and Buddhist India."[5] This was surprising as they could have taken "advantage of the monsoon winds of the South China Sea to transport their influence into Southeast Asia."[6] "It seems plain that the early Chinese were not interested in long-distance maritime trading or expansion overseas."[7] Though it may sound little unbelievable, Chinese cultural influence in Southeast Asia is not present, but only that civilizational influence resulting out of emigration of people had lead to a sort of "cultural island" in Southeast Asia.[8] Issues arising from the migration of ethnic Chinese still persist in the Southeast Asian countries.

In fact in case of Malaysia there are 24 per cent ethnic Chinese. [9] Singapore has eighty per cent of ethnic Chinese. While in Indonesia in a census in 2000 nearly 1 percent-identified themselves as ethnic Chinese though the unofficial figure is assumed to be 3 to 6 per cent.[10] This hesitation in identifying oneself as ethnic Chinese is due to a widespread riots in the 1965. Ethnic Chinese were seen as being conduits of Chinese communist influence. Chinese leadership had consistently tried to use Communist insurgency as a tool for exporting ideology. This acquired a sinister colour especially over its support for the Khmer Rouge, which brutally persecuted people under the policy of imposing primitive communism, in which millions died. China supported this Khmer Rouge government, after the Vietnamese invasion in Cambodia and its dislodgement. Khmer Rouge was pushed to the jungles of Cambodia and Thailand. China continued to support the insurgent movement of the Khmer Rouge. But simultaneously, campaigned against the hegemonic tendency of the Vietnamese government in collusion with the USSR. Simultaneously, China decided to teach Vietnam a lesson for the invasion. This ultimately culminated in the border wars in 1979, but Chinese attempts to teach Vietnam a lesson resulted in "bloody nose".[11] Though, China was supported by Thailand. China also accused Vietnam of acting as Soviet Union's agent to promote its hegemonic interests. While at the same time ASEAN was playing its role in solving issues arising out of the Vietnamese invasion. But no country was willing to side with the discredited Khmer Rouge, China was also having problems over advocacy for Khmer Rouge. It wanted a saving grace exit. The solution to the Cambodian problem became a protracted issue with, involvement of too many powers. While China's Southeast Asia relations came under the influence of many domestic and international developments, internationally end of the Cold war with Gorbachev's policy of *glastnost and perestroika* and domestically China after Mao, pursuing policy of economic modernisation. Now the whole agenda has changed China was looking at economic growth, which has little or no place for, ideological war.

Thus, from 1990s, there was an appreciable change in the China Southeast Asia engagement. In 1991 Foreign Minister Qian Qichen, for the first time attended 24th ASEAN Minister's Meeting as a guest of the Malaysian government. In 1996 it was given the full Dialogue Partner Status. China ASEAN relations have grown since then, presently there are 48 institutional mechanisms managing cooperation between them.[12] Despite the doubts and apprehensions over China's Rise, China-ASEAN relations have progressed well. Similar progress has taken place in the case of bilateral relations of ASEAN countries with China.

China- Malaysia Relations

China-Malaysia relations are one of the good relations between China and ASEAN countries. Malaysia was the first country of ASEAN to establish diplomatic relations with China. The relations had their differences especially over China's support for the Communist Party

Malaysia (CPM). Further there was also conflict over the ethnic Chinese issue, and their dual loyalty, Chinese leadership advised their diaspora to show loyalty to their resident countries. Malaysia has at the same time apprehension of China's rise, but it sees that the prudent way is to engage with China. China and Malaysia economic relations are thriving, with China as Malaysia's fourth largest trading partner. The long term issues are over Spratly islands and China's future behaviour. While on Spratly agreement has been reached between China and Malaysia to solve the problem bilaterally through "friendly consultations and negotiations". While on the larger issue of China rising and appropriate policy responses, Malaysia is more inclined towards China, though at the same time it continues to maintain relations with United States. It has also to do with beliefs in Asian relations, President Mahathir Mohammed, emphasised as against the western dominance. This is one of the strongest convergences between the two, which resonates at the East Asian level as well. As seen in the East Asia Economic Caucasus (EAEC), which China supported.

Malaysia's opposition of making South China Sea as multilateral issue, is seen as China accommodation. Malaysia is said to be following a policy of "limited bandwagoning".[13] Malaysia's overall policy of China, has to be understood in the context of Rise of Asia, where Malaysia desires a closer economic grouping with Asian countries, which cannot be completed without China. In fact, Mahathir Mohammad has been one of the stoutest critics of US policy and Western world, wants to see some sort of Asian Community or East Asian Community coming up in the region, with China as one of the main pillars. Though, military modernisation is one of the worries of the Malaysian government, therefore they are willing to maintain relations with United States, but the safest bet is China adequately socialised into some form of community and CAFTA, is a step in the direction. Malaysia has invested $ 429 million in China, which is equivalent to 9 times investment from China to Malaysia. China Malaysia trade which stood at $ 7.44 billion and now stood at 2009 $ 39.97 billion.[14]

China-Indonesia

Gradual shift has occurred in China and Indonesia relations, the countries re-established a diplomatic relations in 1990, after severance of relationship in 1967. In 1968, widespread ethnic riots took place in Indonesia which killed more than half a million Chinese. The dispute was over the Chinese support for the Indonesian Communist Party and their alleged 'fifth column" activities. This is in contrast to the bonhomie in the relationship between China and Indonesia over the Bandung Conference in 1955. Presently, the relations have not been able to recoup to the same sentiment. Indonesia is apprehensive of the China's rapid growth and military modernisation, but realises that cooperation with China is essential to Indonesia playing important role, in proportion to its size.

With signing of the strategic partnership agreement in the year 2005, Indonesia and China relations have taken a positive direction. A number of agreement on cooperation in many fields have been signed, e.g. in energy, military cooperation. Recently, a Sumdorang bridge has come up through joint efforts of Chinese and Indonesian engineers. Presently, China and Indonesia relations are strategically poised, while it is difficult for both the side to put aside history, but they see their status and role in East Asia or Asia Pacific as quite inter-related, while China would like to have a good relation with the ASEAN's biggest member and possibly the most influential one. While the general belief is that China–ASEAN Free Trade Area (CAFTA), will lead to economic riches of the region, but Indonesia is especially apprehensive because of overlaps with the Chinese industry. Indonesia's dilemma can best be seen in Bert's words, " because of the seeming inevitability of China's increasing power, Indonesia, caught between its distance for close ties with United States and the inadequacies of the subregional defense, has little choice but to engage China and muddle through with what other help it can find to rely on if things go awry."[15]

China-Vietnam

This is one of the most critical bilateral relations of the China in Southeast Asia. Vietnam and China have fought a violent conflict, in late 70s. Vietnam has traditionally followed a policy of fierce independence in the region. China's one of the strongest cultural influence can be seen in Vietnam. Vietnam and China relations in the mid-1970s have competed for regional influence. Now with the demise of Soviet Union and China's rapid rise to global significance, Vietnam is increasingly finding itself constrained. Its traditional rivals for influence in the region. Thailand and Indonesia have progressed while the former has made tremendous economic progress. Vietnam again faces the dilemma of being a neighbour of China, whose economic and military might is appreciating considerably and has limited options, other than engaging it. As with the regional balancer of China, United States it had already fought a war. Therefore, the options of Vietnam are limited. Vietnam owing to historical problems with both the status-quoist power United States and revisionist power China, has no choice to be self-reliant. But Vietnam has moved fast in normalising its relationship with China. In the year 1999, they have entered into signing a Land Border Treaty, signifying Vietnam's eagerness to settle the issue.[16] According to David Kang, Vietnam is pursuing a "nuanced accommodationist strategy toward China which has deep historical roots."[17] By the historical roots, Kang emphasises both the fiercely independent and autonomous character of Vietnamese foreign policy with a quid pro quo in Sinocentric East Asia. It is inevitable, as it cannot rely on United States for hedging, rather it is more likely that providing necessary security benefits it will act as a provocation for China.

China- Singapore

It is the most unequal of the bilateral relationships, while China is a giant and Singapore is a pygmy. But there are many overlapping elements, both are authoritarian governments. But also ethnic Chinese constitute a majority of the Singapore population. Singapore because of being an authoritarian trading state is prefers hedging strategy, whereby it seeks to involve major powers. Singapore's tilt towards United States is quite evident, but it realises that keeping good relations with China is important, especially after its opening up. Singapore cannot military balance China, therefore its focus is on the involvement of China in regional affairs especially through ASEAN. At the same time hedging can be done through having good relations with US, India and Japan.

China-Thailand

Thailand is one of the few countries of the region which has not been colonised. Therefore, it is largely free from historical baggage. It reflects from their foreign policy as well, they have been liberal in their foreign outlook. China and Thailand maintain a good relationship as they were on the same side against Vietnamese invasion of Cambodia. Both the countries jointly helped Khmer Rouge to wage a struggle against Vietnamese intervention. The most important factor affecting the bilateral relationship is that that they are not in conflict over property. Presently, Thailand maintains cordial relationship with both China and United States. Thailand maintains security relationship with United States, "prefers to see it as a balancer in Southeast Asia, the lack of any immediate threats and a view that the US presence in Asia is declining inevitably result in giving less priority to relations with the US."[18]

China and Southeast Asia: Bilateralism vs. Multilateralism

Generally, in China's world view and its preference for a sovereignty and state centric system, therefore it becomes quite understandable that it will prefer bilateral over multilateral. This has been true to much extent in Chinese foreign policy. But this remains central to the Chinese foreign policy imaginings, the question is whether now China is thinking of multilateralism, if yes, what are the factors which are impelling it towards multilateralism? Most importantly drivers are external as well as internal. It is the internal which drives the external. China's opening up of economy in 1978, was the turning point, where trade can't be done in isolation, therefore, it needs at least two parties, but bilateralism in trade is a cumbersome exercise, which involve negotiations, recognising and maintaining MFN status, customs and trade barriers, it goes without saying that China has perfected this riga marole otherwise it couldn't had achieved this burgeoning trade. But the very success of its bilateralism in trade led to many problems like, cumbersome procedure, while with the so called rogue states it involved shady quid pro quo, with US and European countries it had to face many tariff and nontariff issues, like trade labour standards, human rights, and democracy. This was particularly true in case of Sino-US trade which has been the most important component of its trade it was occupying. Ideological shift from bilateralism to multilateralism was taking place, but while economic multilateralism was governed by necessity, security and political multilateralism was guided by, apprehension and caution. First apprehension of being 'ganged up' against, then apprehension of being 'left out'; in fighting both these apprehensions ASEAN was very helpful. If we divide China's multilateralism in these two broad categories, it would be the former which gave China conceptual leap in multilateralism as helpful and beneficial.

While later multilateralism in politico-security context, one can say that it is only means of Chinese national interests as Jing Dong Yuan argues "conditional multilateralism".[19] While it is difficult to see multilateralism vs. bilateralism in a binary, as they both can be used to advance states interests if there was any doubt then China's policy on SCO (Shanghai Cooperation Organisation) would have proved it. Further, the issue is of quality multilateralism, whereas multilateralism has an *ab initio* normative content, diplomatically it is impossible to conduct relations in bilateral level only, multilateralism is an inevitable option, therefore much depends upon quality of multilateralism. Nations show their biases by choosing some multilateral mechanism over others. In case of Southeast Asia, China preferred bilateral over multilateral, friends with Thailand and Malaysia, enmity with Vietnam, economic interdependence with Laos, distance with Philippines, and intervention in Cambodia.

But as it began to open up China found that first it was difficult to deal individually with the countries, as ASEAN had established multilateralism as a pre-condition. China's advantages were over choice of seeing regional periphery with a thriving regional organisation in its southern periphery or countries, which are part of US alliance partner. For China it was profitable to deal with ASEAN, ASEAN way (*musyawarah dan muafakat)* (consultation and consensus) originally derived from Indonesian principles, it did not impose obligations on China. It goes very well with the PRC's reluctant multilateralism. China has acceded to Treaty of Amity and Cooperation, in 2003. ASEAN can claim that it has successfully socialised China into multilateralism.

To some extent ASEAN centrality in the China's multilateralism in the region is well evident. But problem are still over the long term policies of China. China's policy is well over display in its accession to looser multilateralism. But reading motives into Chinese preference for non-binding multilaterals is nothing peculiar to it, as all the great powers have preferred not to pool their sovereignty of action. As, the trend has very often manifested in the United States relations with the United Nations. US has at times refused to defray the expenses of United Nations, where many times Japan has come to its rescue. Further, Chinese reluctance to incur obligations in the regional multilateral mechanism, has been also due to the factor that it was only non-obligatory instruments were on offer. Like in case of ASEAN and its many derivative institutions, they have made their identity in their unique ASEAN way of consultation and consensus. This ASEAN way was said to be behind the success of ASEAN for it helped in transcending the regional divide, otherwise it may have killed the institution from within, as is the case with SAARC. Further it has been asserted that ASEAN way is very much in consonance with the Asian style of diplomacy, which relies on informal networks and negotiations.[20] One of the most cited cases of Chinese unilateralism has been in case of Mekong River Commission, where it is argued that its non-participation is affecting its functioning.

Chinese reluctance of multilateralism is also due to the fact, that if China agrees it will be regarded as the success of the institution and it disagrees it will be seen as yet another example of its intransigent attitude. The later argument is very costly in terms of public perception. This has been one of the major reasons why China has begun to take part in multilateralism mechanism, as non-participation was open to all sorts of interpretation. Southeast Asian states have benefited from the Asian style of quiet diplomacy, when China unilaterally decided not to depreciate its currency in the wake of Asian Financial Crisis in 1997. Now with the economic convergence becoming most important factor, China and ASEAN have entered into a free trading regime, it is likely to benefit former in terms of lessening apprehension.

In case of China bilateral relations is of choice, multilateralism is of necessity. Therefore, this multilateral necessity has to be worked in one's favour. Hence, Chinese preference is for some multilateralism mechanism over others, the most prominent being its preference for Asean Plus Three. It is no significant that its geographical contours are somewhat overlapping with its traditional Sinocentric world. APT process began in 1997, the cooperation is being pursued in 20 areas, with around 57 bodies coordinating cooperation.[21] Apart from the individual benefits of cooperation, it is consonance with larger Chinese aims of a preponderant Asia. It's logical that China will not prefer other states coming into the region, therefore it tried its best to restrict the East Asia Summit. But smaller countries wanted India, Australia and New Zealand to balance China. Similarly China does not prefer APEC as it sees it being dominated by United States. China had apprehensions of the Quadrilateral becoming an incipient containment initiative, which due to other reasons was dissolved because it issued a diplomatic demarche. The apprehensions of China are that no regional mechanism comes up which even in surreptitious way tries to contain its influence in the region.

Despite the acclaimed success of the regional diplomacy, it is generally felt that the region lacks an Asian level of institution to take cognisance of the changing balance of power. That is Asia level security architecture is yet to emerge. Even though many likely metamorphosis candidates exist (ARF, EAS). The reasons are not far to seek as the existing regional atmosphere is too complicated to amenable to a formation of a new institution. Qualitatively the regional balance of influence has changed rapidly to even counterpose a countervailing tendency. It is to the credit of Chinese diplomacy that it has managed to tilt balance of influence in its favour just by following Deng Xiaoping's famous injunctions of "biding time". Chinese diplomacy managed to rapidly respond by changing its growth from 'rise' to 'harmonius growth'. Similarly, in case of China's ascendance as before the policy circles were discussing on appropriate policy instruments to respond to China's rise. China's rise has taken place. The neighbouring countries are already living under shadow of China

The problems which China was facing with US and its South East Asian neighbours, and it's over cautious response to them was being seen as adequate reflection of its tentativeness. The most perceptible change in attitude has come from the United States which from initial hesitancy has come to advocate condominium in the form of G-2. Whatever, natural counter balancing forces could have developed has been pre-empted by multi-focal institutions in the region. This has to do with the centrality of ASEAN, which prides in "process regionalism" than "product regionalism".[22] Thus process was difficult to be meaningful without taking into account changes in regional geopolitics. ASEAN's ravenous search for identity took it to Summit meetings with key regional players China, India, Japan and South Korea. Then, ASEAN Plus Three involving Japan, China and South Korea were appearing to have a greater meaning in economic cohesion. Similarly, the need for a security anchor leads it to form ASEAN Regional Forum (ARF) with twenty seven countries. Over a period of time it was found too bulky to be of benefit. Now the idea was to form a select group of countries which resulted in East Asia Summit.

It is also to be seen that ASEAN is central to institutional imagining of Asia-Pacific. It may be good in giving states a platform to engage. Its efficacy in bringing different countries on the same table, may also become a hindrance in apposite regional institution. Most importantly ASEAN will not be a party to any institutional imagination, which gives it no role to play, it may sound oxymoron in itself. But also at bilateral level the nations, which are part of United

States "hub and spoke" alliance system, have no existential interest to help in spawning of such an institution. Further, countries which are surrounding China will not try to be a party to any such move which is seen as anti-China in any form. It is reflection of contemporary balance of power. Recently, countries lying adjacent to China were non-committal on US participation in Japanese proposal on East Asia Community as they did not want to annoy China.[23] It is here the limits of process is most likely to benefit China. In the recent, US-China Joint Statement emphasised on APEC as the preferred means of economic cooperation in the region and ARF as the forum for regional security issues. In the former India is absent[24], and the later, is too big to produce the necessary security benefits.

China and Southeast Asia: Converging Interests

China and Southeast Asia have developed comprehensive economic relationship. In this it has been helped not only by the territorial contiguity of the territory, but also for the institutional mechanisms of ASEAN. They overlook crucial Sea Line of Communication, which is critical for the Chinese energy supply and energy security. China trade with Southeast Asia countries is substantial and it is growing at very high rate for the last many years. China has recently entered into a Free Trade Area with the ASEAN countries, which will make it the worlds, third largest free trade area.

Table: 4.1 ASEAN's Trading Partners 2008

Partners/ Countries	Exports %	Imports	Total Trade %
ASEAN	27.6	25.9	26.8
Japan	11.9	12.9	12.4
European Union -25	12.8	10.8	11.8
China	9.7	12.9	11.3
USA	11.5	9.6	10.6
Republic of Korea	4.0	4.9	4.4
Australia	3.8	2.2	3.0
India	3.4	2.1	2.8
Canada	0.6	0.6	0.6
Russia	0.3	0.8	0.6
New Zealand	0.5	0.4	0.4
Pakistan	0.5	0.1	0.3
Total Selected Partner Countries/ Regions	86.7	83.1	85.0
Others	13.3	16.9	15.0
Total ASEAN	100	100	100

Source: ASEAN Secretariat available at http://www.aseansec.org/Stat/Table19.pdf.

Though many countries like Thailand and Philippines are a part of the US led San Francisco Alliance. Yet, over the period of time it is generally argued that US hold on the countries is loosening. But even then it can be said many countries due to historical legacy of problems with China, still hold suspicion of its rise. If China's strategy is also to prevent counter-balancing efforts in the region, the South East countries will be easier to persuade. As they are essentially trading countries (see Table 4.2) coupled with a substantial amount of ethnic overlap with China.

Table 4.2: ASEAN Countries International Trade Component

Countries	Ratio of Exports/GDP Year 2008 %	Ratio of Imports /GDP Year 2008 %	Total Trade/ GDP Year 2008 %
Brunei Darussalam	61.9	22	83.8
Cambodia	39.3	39.9	79.2
Indonesia	26.8	25.3	52.1
Lao PDR	15.6	34.1	49.7
Malaysia	87.6	65.0	152.6
Myanmar	24.4	14.0	38.3
The Philippines	29.4	34.0	63.4
Singapore	132.6	126.7	259.3
Thailand	63.9	64.9	128.8
Vietnam	68.1	87.7	155.8
ASEAN	58.5	55.3	113.7

* These data is for international merchandise trade. # Data as of October 2009.

Source: ASEAN Secretariat available at http://www.aseansec.org/stat/Table2.pdf.

Though the organisation had its origin in anti-Communist China environment but it did due to its consensual and non-confrontational processes had led to birth of a special "ASEAN Way". Thus, states with predominant aims of economic growth and development combined together in consensual and accommodative styles are more likely to fall under the Chinese "good neighbour" (*mulin zhengce*) diplomacy. Even though it is in the interests of the countries themselves to engage China, especially for the economic advantages, yet the hesitancy in engaging China has evaporated. They are making all out efforts to reap the economic benefits of China especially in the global economic crisis period. The data of trade for these countries is an ample example of it. China and ASEAN mutual trade is around $ 200 billion.[25]Problems are also there but the countries at the same time are having suspicions on Chinese future role and intentions. Curiously various countries have different security anxieties and consequently they have different ways of solving it. While the continental states like Laos, and Vietnam have no option other than to re-orient their policies towards the bigger neighbour or as some have called it Finlandisation. Laos and Vietnam owing to be territorially contiguous have developed strong economic linkages. Vietnam has signed a boundary agreement where it has accommodated Chinese interests. Laos has developed strong economic and electricity linkages, which make it difficult for it to ignore Beijing.

The other countries like Singapore and Philippines rely on United States for solving much of the anxieties about future China, what is generally being called as hedging. Singapore is aware of the economic benefits offered by China's rise, but is also fearful on China after rise. Therefore, in the region dual policy of economic engagement with China and strategic engagement with United States is the preferred option. With ASEAN and its derivative institutions taking a central role in the regional diplomacy. Singapore is predominantly guided by its national identity of a Global City, and hence become an ideal destination for trade. Historically, it has worked as the entreport of the region. Therefore, its foreign policy is guided towards omni-enmeshment, which China, India, Japan and United States occupy an important part. This has balance of power implications as well, where big powers involvement is likely to balance each other's strategic influence.

While countries like Indonesia, Malaysia and Myanmar are more independently minded. Malaysia and Myanmar has closer relation of the three, thus they have lesser security anxieties about China. Indonesia historically problems with China, when it was giving support to its communist party PKI. Sino-Indonesian relations also struggled with problems over ethnic Indonesians. However, the relations have cooled but the larger uncertainty regarding China's long term intentions and ambitions. Indonesia appreciates China's attempts at cooperating with the ASEAN and its institutions. Indonesia's larger foreign policy is strategically poised as it is the *primus inter pares* among ASEAN countries in terms of size, but is not as Western oriented as Singapore. The later feeling is especially strong after the East Timor independence. Therefore, there is much it has to be felt dissatisfied with, therefore it has a range of options from becoming a rightful member of selective Asia Pacific Community. Therefore in ability to form ideal relationship with either Western countries or China, it has no other choice than to follow policy of engagement with regional stakeholders, without going all out for any one group or country.

While United States continues to be providing of security to countries globally, but it cannot be assumed that it will remain unaffected in changing geopolitical weight of the country. That is United States will be as much affected by the travails of the changes in international politics as the other states. Hence in future it may not be sufficient or willing to balance China. Here role of India becomes important, and it has consciously tried to fill this gap by focusing on Southeast Asian region.

But one of the important means of China diplomacy in the region has been done by ASEAN. It is one of the most successful international organisations of the world. China has not been able to bypass this organisation in its dealing with the sub-regional countries. China-ASEAN diplomacy has been one of the defining features of the geopolitics of the Asia-Pacific. Though China came late to the regional multilateral organisations, but it has adapted itself well to the demands of the ASEAN. The growth in ASEAN- China engagement and qualitative progress has been stupendous. China has acceded to the Treaty of Amity and Cooperation in 2003, the Treaty of Amity and Cooperation enjoins that the signing country will follow the principles of peace and dialogue as enshrined in the ASEAN Charter.

China also prefers ASEAN as its preferred multilateral organisation as already discussed for its characteristic ASEAN way, which promotes consensual decision- making. Also it does not have big powers especially United States, which could have influenced the organisation to forge a counter balancing coalition. For China ASEAN's importance can be gauzed by the fact that China's strategy for the region is focused on ASEAN Plus Three Mechanism. Also, China is the first dialogue country to sign Treaty of Amity and Cooperation. Though China is member of many regional economic groupings like APEC, but its preference is for APT as the regional harbinger of Chinese influence. The predominant aim of China, despite its good relationship with US is that it wants it to be gradually out of Asia-Pacific, as it may limit its influence in the region. Though China openly welcomes the US presence in the Asia-Pacific, it prefers to deal with it bilaterally. Dealing with United States bilaterally has many benefits for China, most importantly in their hierarchical conception of the world, it adds to their stature and prestige. Secondly, the continued US engagement in Asia-Pacific gives security benefits which helps in Chinese achievement of its larger foreign policy goal of peaceful periphery. The smaller states are less hesitant to engage China, in fact this has led to the benefit of the smaller states have shed their reservations in engaging China. This policy has been very successful that it has led to the states going all out to economically engage China. It is also remarked by some that these growing economic convergences are so intertwined that even if the states want to it will be difficult for them to stand against China, without seriously affecting their economic growth.

The growing social connections between China and South East Asian countries are noteworthy. 766 flights between China and ASEAN operate weekly.[26] The tourists from China to ASEAN countries were around 4.47 million comprising 6.9 percent of the total. [27] In the same year 4.98 million people from ASEAN countries went to China. [28]

China's ASEAN Diplomacy

China's regional diplomacy is relied on ASEAN. Both the parties in last one and half a decade have shed inhibitions for each other. For China, the moment of reckoning came in the form of Asian Financial Crisis in 1997. In the financial crisis China didn't devalue its currency as the other South East Asian nations were affected by the devaluation of the currency, owing to capital flight. China seized this moment and gave soft loans to many South East Asian countries, when the help from United States and IMF was reluctantly coming or not coming at all. This has been the defining event in their bilateral relations.

Post-financial crisis both China and South East Asian countries have warmed to each other. While the 1990s was the era of security anxieties over territory and resources, in the post Asian financial crisis the agenda was increasing cooperative mechanisms. They have proliferated increasing ranging from security in the ARF to tourism and epidemics. In their mutual cooperation they have gained in mutual benefits. While the ASEAN countries individually are still sceptical of the China's rise, but they have managed to put up a united front in the ASEAN and able to in myriad institutional mechanisms. ASEAN has been credited with the socialising China into multilateralism and cooperative security. But according to Yuan, "while ASEAN could be credited with socializing China to the concept of multilateralism Beijing embraces remains, conditional, selective, and largely a way to counter US power politics."[29]

It is undoubtedly true that regional atmosphere has improved due to cautious behaviour of China in the regional diplomacy. But it cannot be denied that Chinese foreign policy after the Tiananmen incident in 1989, was coming under widespread criticism and international isolation. It has also to gear its diplomacy to end the isolation and hostility in its foreign policy. Here ASEAN and its characteristic diplomacy of non-interference in internal affairs, came to the rescue of China. ASEAN under its guiding principles has refused to interfere in affairs of Myanmar, even after pressures from international community and United States. Hence, it was unexpected that they will pass any strictures on China over the Tiananmen incident. They maintained a studied silence over the incident where more than 2000 thousand students had died in pro-democracy protests. Thus, ASEAN countries were helpful in getting China out of international isolation. It is no coincidental that China's view about ASEAN is positive, as "however, ASEAN refuses to cater to the seduction of the US and Japan. Instead, it has arrived at a strategic option to breakaway from the patterns of the traditional relationship it entered into with the US and Japan during the Cold War era and embraced the relatively balanced tactics of treading the middle road so as to cope with the transformation and changes that happened to the China-US- Japan relations in recent years."[30]

China also realised that in post-Cold war world when United States is looking to consolidate its "hegemony". It didn't want to come under United States policy of containment. That is it had to act fast to prevent coalition of forces around it trying to contain China. In this aspect the ASEAN was a good instrument. Thus, China began to ride on the sails of ASEAN. Chinese diplomacy in the region has been one of the key reasons for changing of the global opinion of it. Chinese regional diplomacy therefore has been variously termed as "charm offensive". China has signed Joint Statement on ASEAN-China Cooperation Towards the 21st Century (1997), Joint Declaration of ASEAN and China on Cooperation in the Field of Non-traditional Security Issues (2002), Declaration on the Conduct of Parties in the South China Sea (DOC) (2002), Joint Declaration on Strategic Partnership for Peace and Prosperity (2003), and Joint Statement of ASEAN-China Commemorative Summit (2006).

It is not intended to say that the relationship has been one-sided with nothing to gain for the ASEAN countries; they have mutually benefited from trade, in year 2008, the mutual trade has been of US $192.5 billion.[31] China and ASEAN Free Trade Area has been operationalized from January 2009. It is likely to become world's third largest free trade area after EEC, and NAFTA. It will constitute around 1.3 billion people with total GDP of US$ 2 trillion dollars. While the FTA with initial ASEAN countries have become operational from the very first of January 2010, but for the new ASEAN countries like Cambodia, Laos, Myanmar and Vietnam will be operationalized by 2015.[32] The combined population under this FTA will be around 1.9 billion people. The trade among the countries is already very high but it will be difficult to say what will be the future economic effect on the countries, as presently some countries are making positive trade balance with China and other are having negative trade balance with China.[33]

Table 4.3: ASEAN Countries Major Trade Partners

Partners/ Countries	Trade in Billion $
ASEAN	458.11
Japan	211.91
European Union -25	202.35
China	192.67
USA	181.03
Republic of Korea	75.48
Australia	51.59
India	47.46
Canada	10.55
Russia	9.62
New Zealand	7.42
Pakistan	4.84
Total Selected Partner Countries/ Regions	1453.06
Others	257.35
Total ASEAN	1710.42

Source : ASEAN Secretariat available at http://www.aseansec.org/Stat/Table19.pdf.

Chinese reliance on ASEAN is helping advance its geo-economics and geo-politics. The mechanism of the ASEAN has helped to show China that it can be a responsible actor on the international stage. It is willing and able to follow the principles and rules as enjoined in ASEAN institution. While at the global stage US Robert Zoëllick was talking of China to emerge as a "responsible stakeholder" in 2001,

China has already embarked on acting as one in the region. China became a part of ASEAN Regional Forum established in 1994, which was a means of promoting confidence building and preventive diplomacy in the region. The formation of ARF became a geopolitical advantage for the Chinese as it was one of those regional institutions, which were high on formalism and low on content. This very well suited with the Chinese desire to take part in the regional affairs so as to prevent coalescing of neighbouring countries under the new victorious United States. It was also an easy platform for engaging in peaceful diplomacy without incurring any substantive costs. That is one of the cardinal principles of the Chinese grand strategy has been not to let any international agreement constraining its strategic autonomy and choices. Thus the loose regional diplomacy which are more oriented towards Confidence building, are likely to advance Chinese interests, which is aims for a peaceful periphery to grow. But as China grows into a big power it is unlikely that it will still be guided by these principles. Though on the surface it may look that China is well socialised into the regional diplomacy, it is unlikely that same pleasing demeanour will be found in its behaviour once it has attained its rightful position. Thus, the ASEAN may be happy over its own successful history, it is unlikely that will not try to put region into its subordination.

Thus, as the ASEAN website claims, "China supports ASEAN's role as the driving force of the regional processes initiated by ASEAN such as the ASEAN Plus Three (APT) process, ASEAN Regional Forum (ARF) and East Asia Summit (EAS)."[34] But already Chinese efforts to back drive institutional processes and their aims and already evident. China has fervently tried to keep India, Australia and New Zealand out of the East Asia Summit, in 2005, which it had to ultimately acquiesce in the states insistence on inclusion of these states. It has been well known that Chinese desire to make a larger East Asian Community with APT as the central focus.

Riding the sails of ASEAN is only beneficial if the Sino-US relations are managed well. Chinese strategy in the larger Asia-Pacific is thus based on two pronged strategies while bilaterally Sino-US relations has to be given the most priority, at the same time institutionally ASEAN is on highest priority, and strategic acumen will be on how to keep them apart as much as possible. If the Sino-US relations are so managed that other states are not able to exploit the differences between a status-quoist power and revisionist power. It may not go to the extreme of condominium as remarked in Zbigniew Brzezinski term of G-2. This may not seem logical but it is sure that regional countries will take note of the warming of the relationship. As Chinese geopolitical power and weight increases in international system it will not be surprising that China and United States agreeing on a *modus vivendi*.

US in Southeast Asia: Looking Over or Being Edged Out

Traditionally, United States had a dominant position in Southeast Asia. Recently it is being generally argued that United Sates had lost its pre-eminent position in the region. According to Evelyn Goh, " while the current distribution of hard power in favor of the United States will not change for some time, more fluid and challenging is the shifting "balance of influence' in South East Asia with the steady development of China's multilayered relationship in the region."[35] There are contrary opinions as well, which maintain that, " currently, China's growing involvement and influence in East Asian economic and security affairs is not fundamentally eroding the foundation of US alliances and security partnerships in the Asia-Pacific."[36] It is difficult to take a firm view on US presence or absence in Southeast Asia. Some facts are incontrovertible like, withdrawal from Philippines. The most important strategic development has been in the form of Soviet Union's vanishing. Now Vietnam is no longer being able to act as Soviet Union's proxy, due to its own vulnerabilities.

Therefore, region was free for PRC to expand its influence. Therefore expansion comes both at Vietnam's and USSR's expense. On the question of United States, it can be said that absence of US is more superficial and phoney than presence of it is more substantial. Rather polar politics of Southeast Asia is giving China's extra advantages. Under the Bush administration, United States foreign and security policy was focussed on Afghanistan and Middle East, while this region was gradually coming under Chinese influence. In fact, the region's declining importance in the US administration was exemplified when second ASEAN Regional Forum meeting was not attended by Secretary of State Condoleezza Rice in 2007. In the same year President Bush cancelled the first full United States-ASEAN Summit to be held in Singapore.

United States has not been able to counter the Chinese strategy in the region or is practising a sanguine disregard of China's growing influence, and despite its overwhelming military presence it is being seen as losing the region. The new Obama administration has come with this determination to shore up US presence in the region. Secretary of State Hillary Clinton's many tours in the region and Obama visits to the region have shown new urgency in the US to re-assert its prominent position in the region. US has signed Treaty of Amity and Cooperation with the ASEAN. First US-ASEAN Summit also took place in the region. Secretary of State Clinton in a speech in Hawaii, said "United States is back in Asia"[37]

The US regional diplomacy has accelerated, but it is difficult to say that it will be able to recoup its position of eminence in the region. If the Asian Financial crisis of 1997 was the key in determining ASEAN's attitude towards China, it was also determining factor in the US influence in the region. While the response from China was prompt and without any pre-conditions, above all it refused to devalue its currency. The institutions of Washington Consensus, IMF were bureaucratic and dilatory in their response. The help from United States was not as forthcoming. It was one of the features, which shifted regional states opinion towards a regional mechanism for help, which bilaterally came from China, but more importantly, it impelled them towards looking for regional mechanism. The proposal for Asian Monetary Fund, which came from Japan was opposed by United States[38]. Later it began to take shape, with the approval of United States. China and Japan also differ over the regional economic arrangement, while Japan proposes the Comprehensive Economic Partnership in East Asia (CEPEA) comprised of 16 countries, while China favours East Asia Free Trade Area (EAFTA) within the framework of APT.

Thus, in the South East Asian context while China has acquired a benevolent image, with immense economic potentiality, US has become a partner of last resort to help tide over security anxieties. It is not to state that United States economic trade component is less. In comparison to Chinese constituting 11.3 percent of total ASEAN trade, USA's share is 10.6 per cent.[39] The contest over the Free Trade Area is contest between China and its rivals like United States and Japan, as it is aware that "FTAs become important measures for major powers to form communities based on common interests and therefore, China will be in a disadvantageous position in global competition unless it actively engages in free trade with many countries."[40] The fear of China pushing out US in regional economic arrangement is made by Bergstern, where he argues that in future the contest will be over the China led East Asia economic arrangement and US led pacific economic arrangement.[41]

Curiously everybody asserts importance of the United States as a regional stabiliser, even the state which is most likely to be a challenger to its predominant position wants it to stay. As its presence in the region gives other states confidence to actively engage with

China. This development is very much in consonance with the Chinese grand strategy of peace periphery making economic growth possible. But as Avery Goldstein says, China practises strategy with an expiry date, the puzzle is what will be Chinese behaviour once its rise takes place.[42] But it will also be against axioms of international relations that states of an Asia-Pacific system will not adjust their behaviour to changing geopolitical realities. In the Asia-Pacific security complex, it is certain that relative capacities between United States and China, will have to adjust to each others declining and ascending capacities. Other states will have to adjust with this structural change. In fact many states are beginning to do this, like Japan's realisation that in future Japan-US alliance will not be sufficient to adjust to the changing strategic landscape of East Asia. Therefore, the pressure on Japan to Asianise its foreign and security policy. This will have two important consequences one to look for more nested existence in East Asia, or enter into rivalry with China in Asia. In order to hedge its bets, because no one can be sure of China's strategic behaviour it has to simultaneously follow both policies. In the latter case, it will need help of new allies and new mechanisms to safeguard against future behaviour of China.

While US-Japan alliance can continue to be important, one factor which is generally glossed over is likelihood of Sino-US "grand bargain". US-PRC are slated to be competitors and rivals, but what will happen if a grand bargain takes place between the two, as is pointed out in concept of Group of two or G-2. In this the contest will be important but also nature and objective of contest. While the G-2 talks of US-PRC jointly overseeing the affairs of the world, but it ignores individual traits of the countries. China's strategic outlook which is hierarchical and more in align with the particular culture of middle kingdom complex located in East Asia. While the US led West represents universal and globalising traits. In this contest between particular and universal, China through its policy of concessionary balancing will like to restrict itself to East Asia, and letting United States play the global cop. Further, difference between US and China are also of goals, US wants strategic presence so that no "peer competitor" arises, but China's long term goal besides military preponderance is a Sino-centric region with trappings of a community. Japan in its under-normalised state and as Kang says with no desire to play a leadership role,[43] will opt for a nested existence in East Asia.

If the region has to prevent Chinese particularism, then an institutional mechanism is needed which is willing to take declining United States security burden. The ASEAN derivative institutions are inadequate to meet the future challenges from growing China. As Gray Schmitt maintains "The problem with Washington's current approach to Asia-Pacific multilateralism is that it has neither kept up with China's increased levels of engagement throughout the region nor sufficiently kept ahead of that country's growing hard power. The United States has appeared to be a day late and a dollar short in reacting to trends and events in the region. "[44] Somehow, United States is unwilling or unable to meet with challenge, and setting up a new institution which is able to bind the Gulliver can only be a "top down approach". Therefore the Australian proposal of Asia Pacific Community is unlikely to take place, hence "Asia-Pacific's muddled multilateralism" (Schmitt's phrase) continues to occupy our attention.

Conclusion

In the Southeast Asian strategic calculus it is difficult to say who are the losers, but China is the gainer. Its grand strategy of peaceful neighbourhood and economic engagement has come to fruition in the region. Most importantly, despite suspicion of China's future strategic behaviour any credible efforts to ensure future are not taking place. In fact, region is subscribing to the Chinese concessionary balancing. While the states are resigned to gradual accession of Chinese power. Smaller states under the umbrella of ASEAN are vigorously doing what they are best at doing that is creating norms, regimes and principles of international law, especially with China in focus. It is also true that "norms are what bigger states make of it".

Endnotes

[1] https://www.cia.gov/library/publications/the-world-factbook/rankorder/2147rank.html?countryName=Indonesia&countryCode=id®ionCode=eas&rank=16#id. Other members of ASEAN's standing are, (Indonesia, 16: Burma 40; Thailand 50; Vietnam 65; Malaysia 66; Philippines 72; Laos 83; Cambodia 89; Brunei 172; Singapore 192).

[2] Michael R. J. Vatikiotis, "Catching the Dragons' tail: China and Southeast Asia in the 21 st Century", *Contemporary Southeast Asia,* Vol. 25, Number 1, Apri l 2003, p.67.

[3] Wang Gungwu, "Early Ming Relations with Southeast Asia: A Background Essay", John K. Fairbank ed., *The Chinese World Order: Traditional China's Foreign Relations* (HUP, Oxford 1968), p .57.

[4] Martin Stuart –Fox, "Southeast Asia and China: The role of History and Culture in Shaping Futur e Relations", *Contemporary Southeast Asia,* 26, no.1 2004, p.128.

[5] John K. Fairbank, Edwin O. Resichauer and Albert M. Craig, *East Asia: Tradition and Transformation* (London: Geor ge Al len & Un win Ltd., 1973), p . 259.

[6] Ibid.

[7] Ibid.

[8] Ibid.

[9] https://www.cia.gov/library/publications/the-world-factbook/geos/my.html

[10] http://news.bbc.co.uk/2/hi/asia-pacific/4312805.stm.

[11] Gargi Dutt and VP Dutt, *China after Mao* (New Delhi, Vikash, 1991).

[12] Jing Dong Y uan, *China-ASEAN R elations: P erspectives, Pr ospects, and Implications for US Interests*, (Carlisle: SSI, 2006).

[13]Kuik Chneg-Chwee, "The Essence of Hedging: Malaysia and Singapore's Response to a Rising China" , *Contemporary South East Asia,* Vol. 30, No2, 2008.

[14] httpp://english.people.com.cn/90001/90776/90883/7036857.html, accessed on 5th July 2010.

[15] Wayne Bert, *The United States, China and Southeast Asian Security: A Changing of the Guard?* (Hampshire: Macmillan, 2003), p.183.

[16] Do Thi Thuy , The *Implementation of Vietnam- China Land B order Treaty: Bilateral and Regional Implications* (Singapore; S Rajaratnam School of International Studies, 2009), Working Paper 173, 5 March 2009 available at http://www3.ntu.edu.sg/rsis/publications/WorkingPapers/WP173.pdf.

[17] David C, Kang, *China Rising: Peace, Power, and Order in East Asia* (New York: Columbia University Press, 2007), p.145.

[18] Wayne Bert, *The United States, China and Southeast Asian Security: A Changing of the Guard?* p.195.

[19] Jing Dong Y uan, *Asia-Pacific Security: China's Conditional Multilateralism and Great Power Entente* (SSI, Carlisle, 2000).

[20] Hiro Katsumata, " Reconstruction of Diplomatic Norms in Southeast Asia: The Case for Strict Adher ence to the " ASEAN Way", *Contemporary Southeast Asia,* Volume 25, Number 1, Apri l 2003.

[21] http://www.aseansec.org/16580.htm.

[22] Sudhir Devare *India and Southeast Asia: Towards Security Convergence* (New Delhi, ISEAS, Capital, 2006), p.45.

[23] Joel Rathus, " Squaring the Japanese and Australia Proposals for an East Asian and Asia Pacific Community: is America in or out ", November 4, 2009, available at http://www.eastasiaforum.org/2009/11/04/squaring-the-japanese-and-australia-proposals-for-an-east-asian-and-asia-pacific-community-is-america-in-or-out/ accessed on 18th November 2009.

[24] P S Suryanarayna, "Soft Focus on APEC geopol itics", *The Hindu,* November 2, 2009, available at, Http://.thehindu.com/2009?11?02?stories, accessed on November 3, 2009.

[25] http://www.aseansec.org/Fact%20Sheet/AEC/2009-AEC-031.pdf.

[26] http://www.fmprc.gov.cn/eng/zxxx/t653431.htm.

[27] http://www.aseansec.org/Stat/Table30.pdf.

[28] http://www.aseansec.org/24206.htm.

[29] Jing Dong Y uan, *China-ASEAN Relations: Perspectives, Prospects and Implication for U.S. Interests* (Carlisle P.A., Strategic Studies I nstitute, 2006), p.25.

[30] Shen Qiang, "Plur alistic Geopolitics in East Asia Ev olving in Ups and Downs", *International Strategic Studies,* 4th Issue, 2007, p. 51.

[31] http://www.aseansec.org/5874.htm.

[32]http://www.nytimes.com/2010/01/01/business/global/01trade. html?scp=1&sq=China-%20ASEAN% 20Free%20Trade%20Area%20&st=cse.

[33] "China's Economic Power Unsettles the Neighbors", *The New York Times,* December 10, 2009, available at http://www.nytimes.com/2009/12/10/world/asia/10jakarta.html?_r=1.

[34] http://www.aseansec.org/5874.htm.

[35] Evelyn Goh, *Meeting the China Challenge: The US in Southeast Asian Regional Security Strategies* (Washington; East-West Center, 2005), p .ix.

[36] Evan S. Medeiros and others, *Pacific Currents: The Reponses of US allies and Security Partners in East Asia to China's Rise* (Santa Monica ; Rand ,2008), p.231.

[37] Hillary Clinton, " Remarks on Regional Architecture in Asia: Principles and Priorities" available at http://www.state.gov/secretary/rm/2010/01/135090.htm.

[38] Masafumi Iida, "Japan-China Relations in East Asia: Rivals or Partners", Masafumi Iida, eds., *China's Shift: Global Strategy of the Rising Power* (Tokyo: NIDS, 2009).

[39] http://www.aseansec.org/Stat/Table19.pdf.

[40] Iida cites a commentary, which appeared in *People's Daily* on December 15, 2007. Masafumi Iida, "Japan-China Relations in East Asia: Rivals or Partners", p.142.

[41] C Fred Bergstern, *Toward a Free Trade Area of the Asia-Pacific,* Policy Brief PB07-2, February 2007, Peterson Institute of International Economics, available at http://www.iie.com/publications/pb/pb07-2.pdf.

[42] Avery Goldstein, *Rising to the Challenge: China's Grand Strategy and International Security* (Stanford: Stanford University Press, 2005).

[43] Kang, argues that " Japan has historically aligned itself with what it perceived to be the world' dominant power ". David C, Kang, *China Rising: Peace, Power, and Order in East Asia,* p.155.

[44] Gary Schmitt, "A Road Map for Asian-Pacific Security", *National Security Outlook*, available at http://www.aei.org/outlook/100926.

Chapter 5

India and Asia-Pacific: Role and Options

Introduction

Nehru, said, "India, constituted as she is cannot play a secondary part in the world. She will either count for a great deal or not count at all."[1] India's Rise seemingly fulfils the first part of the prediction. Country has entered into a crucial phase in its strategic positioning, which is unparalled in history. While its influence has spread in many parts of the world on many counts (like cultural influences in South East Asia, ideological appeal under non-aligned movement, as in Neutral Nations Repatriation Commission in Korean Crisis), it is in present times that it is likely to emerge as a comprehensive power, with, soft power, high economic growth and military might. While these trends or picture may look appealing at supra level, arrived cumulatively, but are the result of 'top down' approach to assessing India's strengths. As is said, the devil is in details, a 'bottoms up' approach may reveal India's struggle in making gains and consolidating them. The rise of Asia cannot be imagined without India's rise. But India finds itself struggling on many counts. Its rival China is ahead in terms of positioning, trajectory and achievements. Asia-Pacific is the region of choice for China, for India it is a product of natural growth in its position. In short, their vision and means of realising it is different. As already discussed, China's vision is state-centric power/influence maximiser, locked up in relations of competition with United States, while in case of India its vision is a natural product of a democratic country of its size, accentuated by or limited by the democratic character. Democracies tend to be inward looking, people centric and rule oriented. If any vision can be attributed to India's external relations, it is a benign one, focusing on people to people relations, as manifested in diplomatic exchanges, trade relations, and cultural exchanges. While this may be true at general level, India simultaneously is also involved in a struggle for shaping its regional and extra-regional neighbourhood, to advance security and strategic influence.

Indian strategic neighbourhood has become fragile. On the western side Pakistan is fighting an existential battle where the viability of the state has become difficult. After the Maoist takeover in Nepal, the Indian strategic influence is constrained; China has increased its influence in the country. The situation in Sri Lanka is fluid where LTTE is almost finished, it took Chinese help in acquisition of arms and ammunition, showing a growing cooperation between the two countries. China's influence in Bangladesh is increasing. India justifiably feels restricted in the regional context. China has increased its influence in the South Asian neighbourhood. India is discomfited from the realisation that its traditional sphere of influence could be South Asia and even it is under strain. The territorial sphere is constricted but Chinese 'string of pearls' challenges its oceanic spread.

Therefore, India ventures in Asia-Pacific and seeks an appropriate presence. The most important being the Indian attempt to 'look east' in the year 1991. The Indian policy of 'look east' was formulated under the overall pressure of balance of payments crisis. The ASEAN countries were faring very well economically. India in its economic opening, felt that it has missed on the economic success of the Asian tigers, it was imperative that under the liberalisation it should make up for the loss. The 'look east' policy over a period of time evolved into a confirmed policy. The defining aspect of the 'look east' policy is that it has forced India to take a re-look at its sub-continental location and traction.

India's Role

In respect of China's grand strategy of *concessionary balancing* against United States and United States grand strategy of "off-shore balancing." India will find itself with slight leverages which can be had by playing US against China. Rather, the two countries will cooperate to manage the security issues of the continent. While Indian strategic calculation was that it would be supported by the US, which it requested for in a letter by AB Vajpayee to the US President Clinton. It was amply clear that the India's strategic calculation cannot be based on simple equations of the non-aligned world. India is learning the lessons again in the case of Indo-US Nuclear Deal entered into with much elation. Hence, India will have to solely rely on itself in playing the game of power politics within the Asian continent. This will be difficult proposition as the US with its preponderant power and China with its *concessionary balancing* will unlikely to posit sufficient leverages to India to play one against the other. India faces the dilemma of either rising to play power politics at the Asian level or confine itself to be a sub-regional hegemon. India has no choice but to play the role of "swing state" in the Asian geo-politics. It is generally argued that as a "swing state" India will be sought after strategic partner, whose partnership will alter balance of power.[2] Aligning with China will produce a resurgent Asia, or aligning with US will counter China's ambitions.

India's economic growth will put India as the top four economies as predicted by Goldman Sachs Report by 2040 and concomitant military power. Traditionally India has seen its grand strategy functioning under three concentric circles where the first circle is South Asia, our neighbourhood. The second circle is extended neighbourhood which "extends from the Persian Gulf to the Malacca Straits and from Central Asia to the Southern Indian Ocean including all littorals."[3] Finally, the third circle is the global level. Indian foreign policy is calibrated at these three levels. However, in the post-1991 with the putting in place of India's "Look East" policy Indian strategic priorities and policies have begun to take a turn for the better. Now, it is no more straitjacketed in the South Asian region. Initially the "Look East" was a handmaiden of the Indian economic liberalization. It wanted to tap the investment opportunities from the Southeast Asian countries. "Look East" has taken a turn to being a confirmed strategic policy. Now, India takes regular part in the regional security dialogues. India became a member of ASEAN Regional Forum in 1996. India acceded to the ASEAN Treaty of Amity and Cooperation in 2003. India is also a part of ASEAN+6, East Asia Summit and BIMSTEC. India is also part of track two initiatives like CSCAP.

India's look east policy has paid much strategic dividends. In fact, it won't be an overstatement to state that India's perceptible rise in the strategic equations is owing to its rise gaining salience as a balancer to a rising China. States apprehensive to the rising China have actively courted India's participation in the regional geo-politics. Like Singapore and Indonesia played a significant role in getting India into the East Asia Summit. If India seeks to play a major role in the Asian continent it has to redefine its region and consequently its role. A regional power, which was earlier straitjacketed into a sub-region of South Asia due to its obsession with Pakistan. In order, to realise its ambitions of a major power. India has to realise that it has to operate in a regional setting this is a priority as it cannot dissipate its strategic resources in diffuse pursuit of major power and status in the whole globe. Hence identifying a proper regional context is critical, and Asia-Pacific could be this critical context.

In Asia-Pacific, India and China are forming a durable pattern of securitised relationship. In addition to this, Indian economic interests lie in this region. China has become India's number one trading partner. India entered into a Free Trade agreement with ASEAN. In short, the economic potentials of this region is promising. Asia-Pacific accounts for 58 per cent of global GDP, since 1990 it has contributed to nearly 70 per cent of the global economic growth. Apart from economic potential of rising China and need to balance it offers India potential to play the game of "power politics" in the region. As Layne points out "off-shore balancing is a grand strategy based on burden shifting not on burden sharing"[4] Now for India not to proactively act is not the option either India manages to play the power politics in the appropriate context or it will be confined to being essentially a South Asian role. India has begun to play an active role in the Asia-Pacific as discernible from its participation in Malabar-07 exercise involving navies of India, Australia, Japan, Singapore and US. However, it must also be noted "on the cooperative side an off-shore balancing strategy would be coupled with a policy of spheres of influence which have always been an important item in the toolbox of great-power policymakers."[5] Some strains of this thinking can be discerned in the fact that despite being an applicant for APEC membership since 1991 India's membership has been declined twice. Some Indian authors say that APEC is a moribund organisation.[6] Even when countries like Mexico, Papua New Guinea, Russia, Peru and Vietnam have been included in the organisation post India's membership. It is also argued that Western countries do not want India to be included in the grouping.[7] It is to be coupled with the fact that US re-organized its state department recently and clubbed South Asia with Central Asia. It is no secret that US is under pressure in West Asia and once frantically wanted Indian troops for the Iraqi campaign, which India was almost ready to send but for the vehement opposition of the left parties. As Layne points out, " by passing the mantle of regional stabilizer to these great and regional powers, the United States could extricate itself from the messy and dangerous geopolitics of the Persian Gulf/ Middle East and take itself out of radical Islam's line of fire."[8] Thus, the specific injunction in the Nuclear Deal, that India should help in Iran obey the IAEA safeguards, was not only guided by concerns of non-proliferation, but also recognition that India could play an active role in managing the geo-politics of Persian Gulf. But the likelihood of India's potential to play a more proactive role in the Middle East is limited, because of intractability of the region itself but also because of the proclivities to make domestic politics more fractious. Thus, on the cost-benefit analysis, India's more proactive role in the Asia-Pacific region is really helpful. Further, it will prevent being marginalised to a South Asian hegemon. In short, the Indian goal could be to share burden of US in Asia-Pacific than in the Middle East.

This paper is divided into two major parts. The first part, it explores how traditional ways of looking at world and consequently India is mistaken and time warped. Often we look at regional solutions in grand civilisation terms, which are rather part of the problem than solution. Obsession with Pakistan has even limited our view. For, example, till 1990s, Myanmar, with which we share 1400 kms of border was in 'extended neighbourhood' and now is part of 'immediate neighbourhood'. The second part of the paper argues and explores how Asia-Pacific is becoming the *new neighbourhood.* Asia-Pacific is the new neighbourhood, not by virtue, but because India shares land and water boundaries with them.

Table 5.1

India's Trade with Asia-Pacific Countries

In US$ Million

2009-2010 Countries	Import	Rate of Grow-th	% Share of total Imports	Export	Rate of Growth	% Share Export
China	30,824	-5.15	10.6878	11,617.88	24.21	6.4997
Myanmar	1,289	38.84	0.4472	207.97	-6.17	0.1163
Banglade-sh	254.66	-18.67	.883	2,432.51	-2.62	1.3609
Thailand	2,933.25	8.49	1.0171	1,740.16	0.9735	-10.22
Vietnam	521.81	27.69	0.1809	1,838.95	5.77	1.0288
Cambodia	5.05	86.01	0.0018	45.54	2.88	0.0255
Laos	20.05	3,718.-95	0.0070	16.93	88.19	0.0095
Indonesia	8,656.66	29.86	3.0016	3,063.36	19.67	1.7138
Malaysia	5,177.12	-27.94	1.7951	2,835.41	-17.09	1.5863
Philippines	313.07	22.88	0.1086	748.77	0.67	0.4189
Brunei	428.65	7.83	0.1486	24.44	38.57	0.0137
Singapore	6,454.57	-15.68	2.2380	7,592.17	-10.10	4.2475
North Korea	8.71	-84.64	0.0030	422.38	-54.93	0.2363
South Korea	8,576.09	-1.16	2.9736	3,421.05	-13.44	1.9139

2009-2010 Countries	Import	Rate of Grow-th	% Share of total Imports	Export	Rate of Growth	% Share Export
Japan	6,734.44	-14.61	2.3351	3,629.54	19.96	2.0306
Taiwan	2,612.74	-8.93	0.9059	1,877.34	24.80	1.0503
Russia	3,566.79	17.59	1.2367	980.69	-10.55	0.5487
Australia	12,407.-41	11.80	4.3021	1,384.94	0.7748	-3.78
United States	16,981.-92	-8.51	5.8883	19,535.42	-7.63	10.9292

http://commerce.nic.in/eidb/ecntq.asp

GOI, Ministry of Commerce, Department of Commerce

Export Import Data Bank

Reintroducing India in the Region

It cannot be overstressed that the traditional prism of the Indian foreign policy should be re-looked in the contemporary era. Though, the traditional principles give us the veneer of well-guided injunctions but also a means of continuity under whose guidance the foreign policy is formulated and practiced. It is axiomatic that the foreign policy formulation takes place in the overall picture of the strategic culture of the country. Hence, the over-riding need for India re-introducing itself in the regional and cultural context. Some of the salient features of this re-introduction will be a sense of strong break from history both in its negative aspects as well as its purported positive aspects. India does emphasise its helplessness in terms of Pakistan foreign and security policy. Yet, the Indian foreign policy and its strategic culture impel it to counter humongous hate with humongous love. Thus, unrealistic statements and actions come out of our foreign policy behaviour, like PM Vajpayee's visit to Minar-e-

Pakistan, or Advani's visit to Jinnah's mausoleum and calling him secular or unreciprocated unilateralism of Inder Kumar Gujral. The most baffling aspect of Indian foreign policy is the amount of energy, which Pakistan consumes in Indian foreign policy practice. If West sees us in terms of hyphenation with Pakistan, we are too obsessed about it. The second aspect of this fixation about Pakistan is that the Indian foreign policy discourse is almost formulated in response to Pakistan. Though this trend has diminished over the years. In fact Pakistan brings such compulsive hostility that it almost sets the agenda, both when it is strong and now when it is failing. Indian foreign policy is seen as almost continually responding to the Pakistan's foreign policy initiatives. Therefore, the need for re-introduction.

The important question is what are the terms of this re-introduction? One aspect, which the Indian foreign policy most importantly needs to re-introduce itself, is the Indo-Pakistan relation. The most salient term of re-introduction could be *perspective*. The relationship could be put in perspective. Indo-Pakistan relations despite the obsessive nature of their relationship do not have much convergence. Indo-Pakistan trade is miniscule. The tourist flow to each other country is low. Educational exchange is not worth the name. Further, the Indo-Pakistani cultural exchange is significant, yet it is too weak to overcome the atmosphere of hostility. Both India and Pakistan are part of SAARC, yet it has not 'taken off'. Toning down of this relationship could be the most important aspect of re-introducing India. In fact, long-term trends are already underway. Pakistan is identifying with extra-locational Islamic identity of Middle East[9] Most importantly any belief that somehow civilisational logic of culture and community will result in foreign policy bonhomie has not shown in practice. Rather, shared cultural identity has been the problem[10], (South Asia emerging as an epicentre of terrorism is such an example) any belief incorporating them as a solution, risks aggravating the problem. Any belief in this logic does not only extend simplistic logic but also defies the modernist logic of state sovereignty system. Annual report of the External Affairs Ministry espouses the predominant aim of "South Asia as an integrated entity in which there is free flow of goods, peoples and ideas unfettered by boundaries." [11] Similarly, India's other regional bilateral relations are in the need of re-introduction.

India needs to be re-introduced in the region with respect to Indo-Bangladesh, Indo-Sri Lanka and Indo-Nepal relations. One of the avowed principles in which this re-introduction could be made is break from *history*. Further, the overall principle in re-introducing India in terms of these bilateral relations is the realisation that India cannot claim anything as a right, which it has to go through a normal procedure of *negotiation* and *bargaining*. For example, Bangladesh has acquired a new salience in context of 'look east' policy. The Indian assumptions of superior status, automatically transcends into feelings of resistance and disdain by the smaller regional powers. Thus, rather than focusing on building a stable and peaceful relationship, threat of India is posed to invite foreign powers. The strong sense of superiority, which exists in the Indian mindset, coupled with the ethnic and cultural overlaps, creates disarray in the relationship, which neither India nor its neighbours can avoid.

Re-defining the Region

One characteristic, which marks the Indian Foreign Policy, is its global positioning and reach from its very inception. But over the period of time India's legitimate sphere of influence and activity has shrunk. Especially after the Sino-Indian 1962 war, its vision restricted to South Asia. India's positioning shrunk from the global to the regional, especially the 1971 war, entrusted some sort of a regional Monroe doctrine. It has been assiduously maintained in the region, in fact, the Sri Lankan intervention was in pursuance of this policy. Traditionally, India has looked at the world as compromising of three concentric levels.

It is due to this amazing unchanging culture that the India could manage to continue their 'knotty' relationship with Pakistan for more than fifty years, where its diplomatic energy was consumed in countering Pakistani propaganda both at the regional and at the global level.

Globalisation's central idea is de-territorialisation. Though it would be wrong to deny the limits imposed by geography, yet we have to recognise that its limits can be very easily overcome by rapid means of transport. Many plans on construction of a Trans-Asia Highway are recognition of this belief. Myanmar with which India shares nearly 1400 kms of boundary, was in 'extended neighbourhood' till 1990s, now it is in 'immediate neighbourhood'. The strongest representation of the argument can be found in India's 'look east' policy. This policy has naturally evolved with the changing times. That is, the 'look east' policy which has evolved as a result of opening up of the Indian economy with the predominant economic aims has taken a strategic orientation, as stressed by Foreign Minister Pranab Mukherjee, arguing, 'we believe that India's future and our own best economic interests are served by greater integration with East Asia.' [12]

Another way of looking at India is two very commonly used designations, viz., India's immediate neighbourhood and extended neighbourhood. In the traditional conceptualisation of circles, first circle corresponds to India's 'immediate neighbourhood', while second circle corresponds to the 'extended neighbourhood'. The third circle can be taken to mean the global level. Though, at a very generic level it is often argued that Indians do not possess a grand strategy, however, if any grand strategy is found it is largely found in this formulation. The most critical aspect of India's neighbourhood policy is that it stems largely from very loose over-archic Nehruvian principles of universal brotherhood. The aspiration of a common brotherhood in the immediate neighbourhood is not only continuing with the much-arraigned normative and moralistic aims of foreign policy, but also symptomatic of a sense of denial of the historical changes taking place in the sub-continent, viz., emergence of modern state system. It should be noted that in comparison to India, Pakistani elite has been much more mature in adjusting to the partition than has been the Indian ruling elite. It has been more mature in forming long lasting partnerships with US and China.

The naivety is evident of the India foreign policy establishment that at times SAARC's progress is compared with European Union. Consequently many mechanisms to resuscitate the regional economic cooperation structure had failed to take off. Rather, the cooperative structure is hostage to Indo-Pakistan relations. After many failed starts and unrealised potential India began to think of bypassing Pakistan, in any subsequent economic structure, the most prominent being BIMSTEC (Bay of Bengal Initiative for Multi-Sectoral Technical and Economic Cooperation). This regional grouping was formed in 1997 with Bangladesh, India, Myanmar, Sri Lanka and Thailand as members.

It was indeed surprising to note India could not imbibe the logic of Westphalian state system in our immediate neighbourhood. Perhaps this was due to the fact that Mahatma Gandhi, despite being foreign educated could use the traditional idioms to win independence for India. Thus, the Nehruvian elite were in the double bind. While it didn't have the intellectual inclination to break from the traditional idioms, however, on the other hand, it was too Western to imbibe the traditional statecraft of Kautilya. Thus, India, could manage to continue to be obsessed with Pakistan for more than fifty years, and lacking creative ideas to get out of the log jam, which Kapur terms as 'stalemated relationship'.[13]

In it's much of the pre-independence period Indians had very ably imbibed European nationalism but failed to inculcate the Westphalian state system in outlook. This can be traced to the Janus faced character of the anti-colonialism. Even the history of external invasions was converted into a nationalist idiom of vulnerability, internal disunity and disintegration. This could be overcome by rhetorical hyper-nationalism, where emphasis on unity or social integration was a logical option. This strong domestic characteristic was displayed externally as well, where the most pressing ontology was of winning over your enemy. The problem was further compounded by the fact that erstwhile brethrens were now fierce enemies. The belief that thus the more practical aspects of technological backwardness and military strategy were glossed over. For example, in the Battle of Adyar where three hundred Europeans with seven hundred Indians defeated a superior force of more than ten thousand men by the more innovative European military strategy.[14] This inability to see the neighbourhood in state-centric terms, had the logical corollary that we have not yet been able to see our neighbourhood in terms of a balance of power system. This over-dependence on the cultural idioms has prevented the autonomy of strategic studies manifesting in the regional setting. In fact, it was the strategic acumen of the South Asian states, which initiated the formation of the SAARC in the region. India had the apprehension of the states ganging up against it.

Indian policy makers were feeling that the break-up of Pakistan was a vindication of their civilisational logic and were upbeat about the future of Indo-Bangladesh relations. This subsequently proved out to be unrealistic, and now India faces the spectre of an Islamist

Bangladesh, becoming hot bed of terrorism. The civilisational logic was carried to the other extreme in the case of Sri Lanka, where the Indian intelligence was first arming and training their ethnic brethren in Sri Lanka, but were later forced under the strategic logic to fight their own trained terrorists under IPKF (Indian Peace Keeping Force).[15] Even here the intervention was not successful, and the IPKF had to return, subsequently forcing the Indian state to hide behind the traditional foreign policy principle of 'non-interference in internal affairs'. It won't be an over-generalisation to argue that the Indian bilateral relation in immediate neighbourhood had been overtaken by this civilisation discourse; wherever it has been applied it has led to deterioration of the relations. In its immediate neighbourhood, it could be said that India has a successful bilateral relations with the mountain Kingdom of Bhutan, where due to the obvious ethnic limitations this civilisation discourse couldn't be applied. Thus, under the state centric forging of relations had been the cause of success.

The other trend, which has been in practice in India's relations with its immediate neighbour, is 'strategic'. The practitioners of this approach focused on countering every move, step, tactics and sub-tactics of the Pakistani aggression. Because of its origin in the reactive impulses of the region it could not go beyond incremental strategising to the regional impulses. The real problem with this reactive approach was that they were being continually surprised by the strategic developments in the region like increasing Chinese presence. The Indian strategic analysts were while most of the time in self-congratulatory mould, in countering Pakistani tactical moves and counter-moves, but found them out-maneuvered by China, be its rapidly developing border areas through road development. Or Chinese strategic presence in Myanmar or building of a naval base in the Sri Lankan Hambantota. Increasing, Chinese presence in the region was termed as China throwing a 'string of pearls', around India. In fact, China was practicing typical Chinese "foot binding practice" of India in its own regional backyard. India in a misplaced sense of elation found that the country was rising to global eminence, could sublimate its presence from the first circle to second and the third circle. It was unable to realise that the India cannot have a strong base until its regional influence is maintained.

The belief that India as a rising power, is given made India overcome the anxiety of restricting regional presence in the first concentric circle. The interesting thing to note is that while when simultaneously the clamour of India rising was being heard, at the same time the Chinese 'foot binding' practice has become very noticeable in the Indian sub-continent. While the Chinese presence in the region could be traced to the earlier times as early as 1950s in Sri Lanka, while earlier the aims of China was to increase influence, now it has transmuted to a more tangible strategic presence. Pakistan's avowed policy in the region has been to involve as many external players as possible, against India. China in a far sighted move managed to build up strong relations with Pakistan, which was very effective tool in countering India. This was nothing new for India as Pakistan has been avowedly following this practice, of inviting external powers to play a regional role. The 'all weather friendship' between Pakistan and China began to take a sinister trend when China unabashedly helped Pakistan in getting nuclear weapons and missile technology. Indian strategic thinkers had developed a comfort zone where, China could indirectly help Pakistan, but it is unlikely that it will come out into direct military aid. This belief was strengthened in the 1971 war, when despite break up of East Pakistan, China desisted from opening up a second front. Thus, despite the long-term strategic objective of having the military capability to fight a two-front war, we have been able to develop a 'comfort zone', which was very overtly broken in George Fernandes statement in 1998, identifying China as the enemy number one. Gradually, the Indian security establishment began to feel the urgency of the need to counter the growing Chinese threat, which culminated in India's nuclear blasts. The positive externalities of balancing China in Asia-Pacific were beginning to be recognised in the ASEAN neighbourhood.

Asia-Pacific as the New Neighbourhood

India's opening up in the post-1990s, partially enforced by the dissolution of the Soviet Union, made it gradually open up to the Asia-Pacific as the new neighbourhood. It is important to look at the Asia-Pacific level as new neighbourhood, as India in its sense of inordinate importance of ASEAN, may ignore policy formulation at the structural level.[16] Rather, just focusing on ASEAN and its derivative institutions. Even many analysts are noting the inability of ASEAN to deal with geo-political changes in Asia-Pacific. The point very ably brought about by recent postponement of the Summit in Thailand. India has a rich history of cultural influence in the Southeast Asian countries. In the post- independence period India and many Southeast Asian countries established strong links as in Asia Relations Conference 1946 and Bandung Conference 1955. India has been actively involved in the struggle for decolonisation of many Southeast Asian countries. Yet, during the Cold War, being on different sides this history and linkage was neglected. In subsequent period to the formation of the ASEAN India was repeatedly sounded on membership. Its gaze was fixed on the West and hence it continued to ignore.

India opened up to 'look-east' under the overall objective of economic liberalisation. The Indian forays into the 'look east' have primarily piggy backed on the ASEAN. The Indian relations with ASEAN have shown a remarkable progress, starting from the Sectoral Dialogue Partner status in the 1992, to the Full Dialogue Partner status in the 1995. Now the relations have catapulted to the Annual

Summit Level meetings between India and ASEAN, starting for the year 2002. ASEAN has set-up ASEAN Regional Forum (ARF) in 1994 to discuss regional security issues. India has earnestly hoped that its ASEAN engagement will make up for the failure of the SAARC (South Asian Association for Regional Cooperation), and it will be able to convey the image of a responsible actor on the world stage. Indian economic engagement has especially grown in the regional economies. A number of bilateral and multilateral economic instruments have been signed by India with the regional economies and ASEAN. India has been the beneficiary of many instruments coming out of the ASEAN stable, like ARF or most importantly East Asia Summit.

Despite the favourable response of the ASEAN towards economic engagement, it is the ASEAN countries, which have been the regional drivers of the economic, and security initiatives. In one way this has been helpful to India that its external engagement has not been judged with apprehension as was done by its South Asian neighbours, where even mundane economic engagements have been struck down due to the over-encompassing suspicion of India. India has to only say yes or no to the variety of economic and security initiatives by the Southeast countries. The origin of the ASEAN in August 8, 1967, has been to promote regional economic and security cooperation to ward of the threat of communism. The most important contribution of the ASEAN has been to manage to survive and set up a thriving organization in Asia, which has not been replicated.

ASEAN institution is the bureaucrat's paradise, owing to the number of macro and micro-initiatives it takes. The number of the initiatives it has taken has managed to involve countries like India, USA, China, Japan, South Korea and Australia. One of the driving factors of the various economic and security initiatives have been that ASEAN has managed and continues to be the driver of the regional engagements. The question that arises in the contemporary situation is that will that be the sufficient or necessary condition for the regional balance of power to endure. China's rapid economic progress, where it has emerged as number one trade partner of the various countries.

One of the distinct shifts in the regional architecture both security and economic has been in the form of China rising, due to China's rise both economic and security centre of gravity has shifted to China. The regional arrangements have tried to cope up and manage this rise through a number of arrangements like East Asia Summit, ASEAN Plus Three (APT). Yet, as the economic situation changes around the ASEAN countries their incapability to deal with the situation has not changed. Increasingly, the realisation is dawning that ASEAN cannot be an ideal mechanism to deal with the changing security situation in the region. With the recent fiasco the ASEAN Summit in Thailand the unsuitability of the institution has come out in the bolder relief. In fact, by being a regional organization, which is somehow, successful in dealing with the emerging security situation in the Asia-Pacific, it is best providing a means of aggrandizing the Chinese power. In fact, over a period of time it may be able to show that ASEAN and its various arrangements are the best means of delivering Southeast Asia to China.

It should be noted that the China's grand strategy of harmonious development is very much in consonance with the ASEAN objective of economic development and side-stepping major issues of confrontation. It is in this endeavour that China has managed to displace US as the prime economic power of the region. One of the moot points of success of the ASEAN mechanism is that whether it would be enough to manage the changing geopolitical scenario of the Asia-Pacific.

The very policies, which have led to the success of the institution, are also one of its drawbacks. ASEAN'S avowed principle of non-interference in the internal affairs, has led to show that inability of ASEAN most prominently Myanmar issue. Or its focus on economic integration. It won't be an exaggeration to say that almost exclusive focus on the economic integration has China as the unintended beneficiary. It provided China to practise its economic diplomacy unhindered and quite at ease. Chinese regional economic diplomacy has been described as China's "charm offensive" or "China fever". China's strategy of economic growth is matched by ASEAN's promotion of Free Trade Area. As a consequence of which China has managed to become number one trade partner of many countries. It has promoted regional economic arrangements like GMS (Greater Mekong Subregion). In fact, the effect has been that the China has become the regions economic locomotive. The present situation is very beneficial to China as it very aptly matches with Deng Xiaoping's injunction of 'biding their time'. The general tendency to look at increasing Chinese involvement in the regional economic arrangements as an example of hedging may not give complete picture. China has also to look that its, overall aim of East Asia Community (EAC) is not led by Japan or by US under the overall Asia Pacific Community. Particularly, after the global economic crisis, China will want to lead the East Asia Community, and ASEAN'S driver role helps preclude leadership of Japan or any other power. As Bergtsern maintains that, "the systemic issue is the potential clash between a China led Asia and a US-led "West" for leadership of the global economy."[17] In this objective ASEAN is the ideal mechanism, which is unlikely to raise suspicion, invite other powers to take part in the regional integration. China vetoed the idea of Asian Monetary Fund in 1997, to prevent the Japanese leadership in finance. Simultaneously, China went a step ahead, after acceding to the WTO, even before Japan and South Korea in negotiating Free Trade Area with ASEAN. India wants to be part of the East Asian economic growth story, China disapproves the Japanese idea of East Asia involving 10+3+3, while China wants it to stop at 10+3. India would like to convert the East Asia Summit membership into the East Asia Community, which could ultimately become Asian Economic Community.[18] The growing economic integration will affect the larger politico-economic security environment of the Asia-Pacific. China officially maintains that the US is welcome in Asia-Pacific.[19]

This may not be a grudging acceptance of the US role, in fact it best works to the advantage of China. As US presence in the Asia-Pacific soothes the anxiety of smaller powers of the region, they are free to engage with China economically. In such a context ASEAN with its variety of security initiatives, manages to keep the regional security atmosphere peaceful.

The critical question is whether, the security initiatives established under the overall rubric of ASEAN, will be able to deal with an assertive China. The overall Chinese Grand strategy has been to focus on economic development, and restricting from taking pre-mature leadership, as has been enjoined in Deng Xiaoping's famous injunctions. China's close economic relationship with most of the ASEAN members is well noted. Though, according to some estimates China's influence has not spread to such an extent that it exercises preponderant influence on the countries policies.[20] Though, ideally the states in concern would not like to face a situation where they have to choose between the two powers viz., China and US, yet the situation is like growing convergence between the two powers is that the states have begun to take into account the preference of China in their policies. Many states of the region who have defence partnership with the United States, yet as the push comes to shove it will be difficult to say to which side they will tilt. Further, it must be asserted that if China has any worldview it is in its traditional middle kingdom complex, where the regions surrounding it owe a special obligation to it.[21] Thus, the likelihood of China able to adopt universal benign policies is difficult to assert. Therefore, the imperative of guarding against China. The regional security arrangements are inadequate to guard against an assertive China.

A stable balance of power mechanism in the Asia-Pacific is necessary for India, as it has already fought a war with China in 1962. It is unlikely that the rivalry between the two powers would subside. India is essentially looking for a way out of the straitjacket of South Asia, and Asia-Pacific provides the requisite gateway. India wants a strategic presence and role in the Asia-Pacific, which China would like to deny India. As it is in the interests of the many Southeast Asian countries to counter China, they are insistent on inviting India in the regional fold. The most important role in this context has been played by Singapore. After India's display of open interest in ASEAN Singapore has played a key part in getting India into many regional instruments. The most important being the East Asia Summit, where China was opposing inclusion of India into the Summit, Singapore actively pushed India's case for inclusion.

India's economic integration with region has progressed satisfactorily through a variety of instrumentalities. Yet we cannot see region predominantly in terms of economic integration. This is the risk with making ASEAN as the fulcrum in its regional diplomacy. Despite the stupendous economic achievements made by ASEAN countries it will be erroneous to disregard its limited role in terms of regional security architecture, even if they have spawned a number of regional security initiatives like ARF. The predominant small state composition of ASEAN is well suited for providing platform for states to discuss on regional security situation. This is the reason why states baffle in providing adequate responses in the context of security exigencies, like clash over South China sea territories. In these case it becomes one-to-one issue or in the case of China.

The major benefits of the economic integration of East Asia are self-evident. Some of the highest growing countries parts of the region like Japan, South Korea and Taiwan. China is actively taking part in the regional growth story, its economic diplomacy especially after the global economic crisis, has led to accretion in its soft power. It is especially pertinent to note that the India's ability to play a role in the Asia-Pacific region will crucially depend upon its bilateral relations with key countries of the region, most importantly being China and United States.

Table 5.2

India's Top Twenty Trading Countries
(in US $ Million)

Rank	Country	Export	Import	Total Trade
1.	U ARAB EMTS	23,970.22	19,500.73	43,470.96
2.	CHINA P RP	11,617.88	30,824.04	42,441.92
3.	U S A	19,535.42	16,981.92	36,517.34
4.	SAUDI ARAB	3,906.71	17,097.57	21,004.28
5.	GERMANY	5,412.86	10,318.85	15,731.71
6.	SWITZERLAND	589.38	14,698.47	15,287.85
7.	SINGAPORE	7,592.17	6,454.57	14,046.74
8.	AUSTRALIA	1,384.94	12,407.41	13,792.35
9.	IRAN	1,853.17	11,540.85	13,394.01
10.	HONG KONG	7,887.81	4,748.15	12,635.96

Rank	Country	Export	Import	Total Trade
11.	KOREA RP	3,421.05	8,576.09	11,997.14
12.	INDONESIA	3,063.36	8,656.66	11,720.03
13.	U K	6,221.32	4,461.83	10,683.15
14.	JAPAN	3,629.54	6,734.44	10,363.98
15.	BELGIUM	3,759.26	6,019.21	9,778.47
16.	KUWAIT	782.45	8,249.49	9,031.94
17.	NIGERIA	1,408.67	7,287.91	8,696.58
18.	NETHERLAND	6,397.53	2,130.00	8,527.54
19.	MALAYSIA	2,835.41	5,177.12	8,012.54
20.	FRANCE	3,819.74	4,192.40	8,012.14

Source http://commerce.nic.in/eidb/iecnttopn.asp

Government of India, Ministry of Commerce, Department of Commerce

Sino-Indian Relations and Asia-Pacific

India is a natural rival of China in Asia. India and China relations have taken a turn towards better in recent decades, yet suspicion between them two sustain. It is unlikely to go away. This relation will be crucial for India to handle, and how it handles it will guarantee its future. In the Buzanian sense China holds the enmity pole in the Asia-Pacific security complex.[22] In fact, this is not the ideal picture as China is slated to become India's number one trading partner in the near future. It is unlikely that India can partake of the regional economic pie bypassing China. Sino-Indian relations constitute an integral part of its Asia-Pacific role projection. It is important that India handles its role with utmost care. It will be unhelpful if the relation tilts either way, if the relation becomes too warm, then India risks the relation of becoming one sided, and open to the accusation being state of China. Too much closeness with China will the leverages, which it has with China's disaffected neighbours. Now if the relationship becomes too hot to handle, it will affect entire Indian positioning in the region. India will not be able to match the leverages, which China can bring to the table. Yet it is also undeniable Sino-Indian relations are made up of natural rivalry. India will have to juggle the relationship in such a way that the relationship doesn't worsens from rivalry to the level of adversary and doesn't becomes too close to become an ally. At the conceptual level this has to be kept in mind as the latter option is quite unlikely. Yet even a loose handling of the relationship in first context will lead to the loss of status and diverting for its path of economic growth and strategic consolidation.

The Sino-Indian rivalry is also gives India strategic leverages. In case of many Southeast Asian countries, which are suspicious of the Chinese geo-strategic intentions, are eager to invite India in the regional fold. One country whose contribution in not only paving the way for India in the regional context but also clearing the path ahead. Singapore's role in augmenting the role of India is immense. After India showed inclination of accessing to ASEAN, progressively got significant entry into the region. In fact, India was accorded Dialogue Partner Status earlier than China, which has been active in ASEAN much earlier than India, which was active from the 1992, when it was accorded Sectoral Dialogue Partner Status. China was miffed at this priority given to India in the ASEAN. Once again China didn't wanted India to be part of the 16 nation East Asia Summit. Yet countries like Singapore, Indonesia, Malaysia and Japan actively advocated India's case. A better perspective in the case of India's gradual entry into the new neighbourhood, can be gleaned from the fact that traditionally Asia has been regarded as extending from New Zealand to Thailand, not even Myanmar was considered part of the Asian spread, it was only later that Myanmar got entry into ASEAN. Yet in the last seventeen years India has been successful in redefining its new neighbourhood. It could not have been possible without the efforts of the key Southeast Asian players. India's 'look east' policy has managed to give India both its economic and strategic deliverance from confines of South Asia. This is the new neighbourhood where India and China will also seek to contest. From China's strategic interests and its tradition of the middle kingdom complex, it will be more suitable that the role of players like India and United States are restricted if not entirely capped altogether. In the case of former it will try to use diplomatic power, while in the case of later China will try to limit US's role by 'fraternal embrace'. China's overall grand strategy of harmonious development precludes any assertion of its military power. Rather only occasional testing of the mettle as was done in the case of recent naval sparring incident in South China Sea.

Sino-Indian rivalry is extending in case of naval expansion. Chinese 'string of pearls' is constricting India's role in the Indian Ocean. China plans a massive extension of naval capabilities as shown in the recent naval meet at Qingdao where navy from fourteen countries were represented. Pentagon in its Annual Report to the Congress noted the continued expansion in the Chinese defence preparedness, with 'beginning to articulate roles and missions for the PLA that go beyond China's immediate territorial interests.' With the planned acquisition of the aircraft carriers its dominance will be established. China's preponderant aim is to thwart any attempt of outside power to military help Taiwan, in case of its declaration of independence. As, China has not renounced use of force in unification with Taiwan.

Sino-Indian relations will much depend upon the role of the United States in the Asia-Pacific. Many times question has been raised over the reducing role of the United States in the Asia-Pacific. It was pointed out that US focus is on the Iraq and Afghanistan. Even the Southeast Asian states were pointing to the neglect of the US, which it tried to correct by appointing an Ambassador to the ASEAN. The recent visit of the new Secretary of State Hillary Clinton to Asian countries corrected this tilt. She argued for a 'comprehensive partnership' with the China. The common refrain from the US policy circles is that the US is the resident power of the Asia-Pacific. It is defence allies to countries of the region, viz., Japan, South Korea, Australia, Philippines and Thailand. Singapore and New Zealand is also close ally of the US in the region. China has asserted that it welcomes role of the United States in the Asia-Pacific. This may not be entirely a grudging acceptance of the US power and reach in the continent. It is true that ultimately China will want to be the dominant power in the Asia-Pacific. Yet the present situation and for a long time to come it doesn't want its policy of harmonious development be disturbed by any attempts to take pre-mature leadership in the region. US presence adequately helps in this grand strategy of free riding the order in the Asia-Pacific.

The key states of the region are more focused on availing the economic benefits of China's growth, and they would like to hedge against its military superior neighbour. The alliance and defence partnership with US provides them with adequate assurance in exploring the economic relationship. The presence of the US in the regional security discourse provides the regional countries much needed confidence to engage with China. China's overall objective is to accentuate the decisional dilemmas of the regional countries in a situation of having to make a choice between US and China. Though, the regional countries would not like such a situation to arise, yet their behaviour would be difficult to predict in case of such an occurrence.

However, it is not that the variable of US-China relations will continue to be of status-quoist vs. revisionist power. It will be difficult to say that whether China is a conservative power or revisionist power, owing to the long time horizons of its defence and security policy, it may well fall in between the revisionist power and status-quoist power. China has undertaken a fairly patient endeavour in building its relation with the United States. Thus, the realist predictions that peaceful rise of new powers will not take place. What we now see is the gradual convergence in the views of United States and China, especially after the global economic crisis.[23] China has bought up more than $1.9 trillion dollars in US treasury receipts, pointing to the growing global interdependence between the two. Like in the recent defence talks, which were held up, were termed as the "best talk in decades".[24] Secretary of State Hillary Clinton has repeatedly announced that Sino-US relations are the most important relation. The strategic thinker like Zbigniew Brzezinski asked for an informal G2 between the two countries. In an article, China expert David Shambaugh points out the areas of convergence between the two countries. China and US have identical views in many of the areas.[25] Robert Zoellick's idea of responsible stakeholder has begun to take a firm root in Chinese behaviour. China is actively showing interest in order maintenance in key areas like, Southeast Asia financial crisis, recent stabilisation fund after the economic crisis, and offers of aid to tide over the balance of payments crisis in East Asia, initiatives like Chiang Mai Initiative.

India and other Powers in Asia-Pacific

The corollary of the Indian engagement with ASEAN has been that its bilateral relations with the countries have distinctly improved. India's best relations in the region have been with Singapore. In fact the role of the Singapore in facilitating Indian forays into the Southeast Asia is prominent. It played an active role in India's entry into ASEAN, ASEAN Regional Forum, India-ASEAN Summit and East Asia Summit. Singapore was suspicious of China and decided on fully engaging India. Singapore is the pivot of Indian engagement in the Asia-Pacific.[26] India and Singapore relations have strived on all levels of spectrum. India's economic engagement with Singapore is the highest in the region. After signing of the CECA (Comprehensive Economic Cooperation Agreement) in year 2005, the trade between the two countries have jumped from US $11.9 to 25.8 billion in US $2008 billion. It is one of the largest investors in India. India and Singapore have working defence relationship as well. One relationship, which has frustrated India's ambitions in the South East Asia, is Myanmar, which poses challenge to India not only for its growing closeness with China, but its insular policies and anti-democracy policies. India's feeling of the strategic encirclement has tapered down due to India taking a series of steps to correct Myanmar's governments tilt towards China. Yet the feelings of being a junior partner in terms of influence in Myanmar persist. The problem with Myanmar is that its insular policies have restricted India's opening to the Southeast Asian countries. While it's anti-democracy stance in putting Aung San Su Kyi under detention, opens India for criticism for engagement with the Military Junta. In terms of cost benefit analysis, India's engagement has only managed to assuage its sense of feeling of being outmaneuvered by China in its own backyard. The need for a landlink to the Southeast Asia has become increasingly important. Myanmar occupies key place in its two regional initiatives like BIMST-EC and Mekong-Ganga Co-operation.

Indo-Myanmar's Friendship Road connecting Tamu to Kalemyo and Kalewa, is the step in providing this connection across the highway. Myanmar has not fulfilled its obligation to extend the Kalewa road to Mandalay, rather the military elite sees more interest in the opening on the Yunan province of China.[27] Apart from Myanmar, and Singapore, the other country, which holds potential for India in Southeast Asia, is Vietnam. India's advantages in terms of Cold War engagement have led to the unrealised potential of the relationship. Vietnam's difficult history with China notwithstanding, it has little choice other than compromise with the reality of China's preponderance especially in terms of economic engagement. China and Vietnam have solved the border issue mutually. India and Vietnam have developed a defence partnership with the country. Though India's Vietnam engagement is proceeding on various initiatives like hydrocarbons, human resources development and soft loans. India's relations with Thailand have been very successful, especially its corresponding 'look west' policy. India and Thailand signed a Framework Agreement for FTA in 2003. India and Thailand economic relations have been successful, yet the full potential has not been realised.

Indonesia is the largest country of the ASEAN, possesses largest number of Muslims. Coupled with the fact that it's a democracy it adds to attractiveness. Hillary Clinton's chose Indonesia as one of the stops of his maiden tour to Asia, re-emphasised its importance in the regional fold. In fact, in ASEAN it is a big country among small powers, it is also being realised that Indonesia is not able to exercise influence according to its strategic weight. In case of Indonesia the feeling is that with ASEAN as its central focus of foreign policy, its agenda is limited by weaker powers.[28] Recent cancellation of the East Asia Summit in Thailand, is a case in point. Rizal Sukma called for a formation of Asia-Pacific 8, involving countries like US, Japan, China, India, Russia, South Korea, Australia and Indonesia.[29] In

Indonesia a realisation is dawning that their worldview is limited by the ASEAN'S centrality in their focus policy, and are notable adequately to focus on Middle East countries. The desirability of new security architecture is also emphasised by Australian Prime Minister Kevin Rudd, calling for an Asia Pacific Community.[30] Australia notes the strategic uncertainty accentuated by global economic crisis in the recent *Defence White Paper* 2009. It is also worth noting that perhaps China is the only country in the global economic crisis, which is likely to emerge stronger.[31] As White asserts, " and the long term effects of the crisis could amplify, rather than reverse, the long term shift of economic, political and strategic towards China."[32]The Defence White Paper does accept the criticality of continued US involvement in the Asia-Pacific, yet statement on China is worth noting, it encapsulates: *China's political leadership is likely to continue to appreciate the need for it to make a strong contribution to strengthening the regional security environment and the global rules based order.* [33] The ambivalence in White paper reflects the economic predicament of Australia, which recognises that China has become Australia's number trade partner from 2007. The criticality of China in Australia's economic growth in the times of recession becomes very important. Australia would not like to choose between US and China rather recognises US as the ally and China as a partner. Even Kevin Rudd the new Prime Minister is ridiculed for very overt pro-China position. Some analysts see even the Australian idea of Asia Pacific Community as a means of balancing China. It is difficult to predict on which side will be Australia. Gradual realigning of the region with China as economic centre in the Asia-Pacific is worth noting. India's relationship with Australia is especially economic relations, where India eyes natural resources from the country. Australia and India cooperated on Quad and Malabar exercises in 2007. Australia supports Indo-US nuclear deal, and agreed to supply Uranium to India, later rescinded its promise. This is a policy change from its opposing sale of Uranium to India for not signing NPT. India and Australia have also signed an MOU on defence cooperation. Yet apart from the future potential of micro-initiatives one cannot ignore the fact that strategic behaviour of Australia and Japan will be more governed by the larger systemic pressures of Asia- Pacific. The ambivalence in the policies of Australia will be interesting to watch in the case of growing closeness between US and China. Australia will be under no pressure to enlist the support of other powers like India, Singapore, and Japan. Indo-Japan relation will be also governed by the larger dynamic of systemic level pressures.

India and Japan relations have improved, after the rapid progress of relations between India and United States. Japan had adopted a strong position on India's non-signature of NPT. This became more hardline after the atomic blast of the 1998. As the relations between India and United States began to warm, Japan didn't wanted to be left out, therefore its approach began to change. It also wanted to increase relation with India to counter the rise of China. India and Japan signed an 'Eightfold Initiative for Strengthening Japan-India Global Partnership' in 2005. A number of High Level visits between two countries, after 2000, suggest the growing convergence between the two countries. Despite the increasing interconnection between the two countries the relationship has limitations. Japan is influenced by the US approach to the country. Secondly, its interests in taking part in the economic opportunities in China are strong. For example Sino-Japan trade in 2006 stands at near $207 billion, while Indo-Japan trade stands at $ 6.5 billion. Yet, "strategically, India and Japan share such regional and global objectives as ensuring maritime security in the Indian Ocean, controlling the proliferation of WMD, countering terrorism, and balancing against the rise of China in the Asia-Pacific region."[34]

Conclusion

In Indian foreign and security policy Asia-Pacific is emerging as the 'new neighbourhood'. The realisation that India's quest for great power status can only be realized in the new neighbourhood is gradually taking firm root in nations thinking. This neighbourhood will not only have India's number one adversary but also in its number one trade partner. The most interesting thing is that, these two will coalesce into one. China is slated to become India's number one trade partner by the end of 2010. In this context of interdependence, India will have to face with entirely different category of challenges in formulation of foreign policy. Now it is no longer the simplistic paradigm of either friend or enemy. In fact, in case of China it will be both. After hurtling through a number of policy options, US is willing to recognise China as the most important power. In this strategic development a fairly complex challenge presents to Indian foreign and security policy practitioners, where we cannot rely on entirely rely on US to balance China. The response has to be multi-variate and along a broad spectrum of policy choices. The look east policy is one and fairly successful at that, yet India has to look at the structural level as well. China with its economic integration with ASEAN, US with its defence allies, coupled with the increasing interdependence between US and China over the global economic crisis are in a comfortable situation in the Asia-Pacific. India may be counting on small nations in its attempt to balance at structural level, which may be insufficient, even Indonesia is beginning to realise. Australian PM Kevin Rudd's proposal of Asia Pacific Community was an attempt at such a direction. It is beyond saying that Indian economic engagement comparatively is small, and it needs to be increased. Indian look east policy has been very successful, yet the need to realise its limitation is imperative. India has to operate at systemic level, to play a commensurate role in Asia-Pacific.

Endnotes

[1] Jawaharlal Nehru, *Discovery of India* (New Delhi: Oxford University Press, 1998(1946)),p.56.

[2] C Raja Mohan, "India and the Balance of Power", *Foreign Affairs,* July/ August 2006.

[3] Satish Nambiar, "A Role for India in the Emer ging World Order", *USI Journal*, July-September 2006. p.343.

[4] Christopher Layne, "Offshore Balancing Revisited", *The Washington Quarterly*, Vol. 25, No . 2, Spring 2002, p .247.

[5] Ibid., p.246.

[6] PV Rao, *India and ASEAN: Partners at Summit* (New Delhi: Knowledge World Publishers, 2008).

[7] Bhanoji Rao "Does APEC Membership Really Matter for India" http:// wwwthehindubusinesslinecom/2007/01/23/stories/2007012300050800'htm.

[8] Christopher La yne, "Offshore Balancing Revisited",*The Washington Quarterly*, Vol. 25, No . 2, Spring 2002, p 246.

[9] S Akbar Z aidi, 'South Asia? West Asia? P akistan: Location, I dentity',*Economic and Political Weekly,* Mar ch 7, 2009, V ol. XLIV No 10. Z aidi ar gues, " Whi le Pakistan's location has not shifted in the last 36 years...there has been a marked shift in terms of identi ty and association", p.38.

[10] Sikri blames "the baneful effects of the politics of cultural identity" for India's problems with its neighbours. Rajiv Sikri, *Challenge and Strategy: Rethinking India's Foreign Policy* (New Delhi, Sage, 2009), p.16.

[11] MEA Annual Report, p.i.

[12] Pranab Mukherjee's address " India's Look East Policy" at the Institute of Foreign Affairs and National S ecurity, Republic of Korea, on 17th October, 2007, available at, http://meaindia.nic.in/index.htm.

[13] Ashok Kapur, *India from the Regional to World Power* (New Delhi: Routledge, 2006).

[14] Geoffery Parker, *The Military Revolution: Military Innovation and the Rise of the West, 1500-1800* (Cambridge: Cambridge University Press, 1996), pp.133-134.

[15] According to B. Raman, "Reports of the sufferings of the Sri Lankan Tamils at the hands of the Sinhalese moved her [Indira Gandhi] to go their help. The R&AW was asked to start an activist policy in Sri Lanka to assist the Sri Lankan Tamils." B. Raman, *The Kaoboys of R&A W: Down Memory Lane* (New Delhi: Lancer, 2007), p .124.

[16] Naidu argues 'since there is no tangible evidence to suggest that India has factored in the dev elopments at the Asia-P acific level to formulate its policy, it appears the Look East pol icy, as it has been f ollowed since its initiation in the early 1990s, is primarily focused on S outheast Asia.' G.V.C. Naidu, 'Whither the Look East P olicy: India and S outheast Asia',*Strategic Analysis*, Vol.28, No.2, Apr-Jun 2004.

[17] C. Fred Bergstern, *China and Economic Integration in East Asia: Implications for the United States* Policy Briefs in International Economics, Number PB07-3.

[18] Nagesh K umar "India and br oader economic integr ation in Asia", in *Indian Foreign Policy: Challenges and Opportunities*

[19] 'China welcomes r ole of US in Asian-P acific Area", *China Daily,* February17, 2009, av ailable at http://www .chinadaily.com.cn/china/2009-02/17/ content_7485786.htm.

[20] Evan S. Medeiros and others, *Pacific Currents: The Responses of US Allies and Security Partners in East Asia to China's Rise* (Santa Monica, Rand, 2008).

[21] Kishore Mahbubani, argues that "(But) China lacks a vision for the world... (Given these overwhelming domestic concerns) Chinese leaders have little appetite to lead the world. " Kishore Mahbubani, The *NewAsian Hemisphere: the Irresistible Shift of Global Power to the East* (New York: Public Affairs, 2008.), p.239.

[22] Barry Buzan and Ole Weaver, *Regions and Powers: The Structure of International Security* (Cambridge: Cambridge University Press, 2003).

[23] 'Crisis could be 'turning point ' for Sino-US ties',*China Daily,* March 02,2009, available at http://chinadaily.cn/china/2009-03/02/content_7525023.htm.

[24] Xiaohuo, Cui and Peng Kuang, "China-US defense talks best in decades" , *China Daily,* March 02-2009, ht tp://www.chinadaily.com.cn/china/2009-03/02/content_7524246.htm.

[25] David Shambaugh, "China Engages Asia: Reshaping the Regional Order", *International Security,* Vol. 29, No .3, (Winter 2004/2005).

[26] Vibhanshu Shekhar, *India- Singapore Relations: An Overview, IPCS, Special Report,* No. 41, June 2007 .

[27] Reneaud Egretau, "India's Ambitions in Burma: More Frustration Than Success?"

Asian Survey, 48, 6, 2008.

[28] "Indonesia told to initiate new Asia-Pacific Forum", *The Jakarta Post,* 6 May 2009.

[29] Ibid.

[30] John Chan, " Australia Call for "Asia-Pacific Community": A Sign of Growing Tensions" *World Socialist Website,* www.wsws.org. 27 June 2008.

[31] "China's economic growth and the present economic crisis operate on very different timescales." Hugh White, *A Focused Force: Australia's Defence Priorities in the New Century* (New South Wales, Lowy Institute, 2009), p.2. Also see

Mathew J. Burrows and Jennifer Harris, 'Revisiting the Future: Geopolitical Effects of the Financial Crisis', *The Washington Quarterly*, 32,2, 2009.

[32] Ibid., p.2.

[33] *Defending Australia in the Asia Pacific Century: Force 2030,* Defence White Paper 2009, p.34.

[34] Madhuchanda Ghosh, "India and Japan's Growing Synergy: From a Political to a Strategic Focus", *Asian Survey,* 48, 2, 2008, p .301.

Chapter 6

Conclusion

China's rise is the important strategic development taking place in the Asian neighbourhood. It will have far reaching implications on the global geopolitics. But for the Asian countries like India, Japan, Russia and Indonesia they will be historic, historic for the opportunity grabbed or missed. While we are still struggling to know the implications of China's rise, for the Asian countries, the rise will be closely felt at home, than just being part of a global chessboard. Apart from the unhelpful dilemma of China benign and China belligerent, the most important factor is that China has decided to wait, to wait for its grand strategy to fructify itself. The sine qua non of any nations grand strategy is that it aims to make the state economically powerful and military strong. This is one of the axiomatic principles of the international relations which holds true across theoretical boundaries, of realism, neorealism, constructivism and neo-liberal institutionalism. Though, their precise expression may vary. Coupled with the Chinese ascendance is globalisation, while in the interrelated and complex affairs of international politics it will be wrong to over-emphasise one development over the other. China's rise is amidst and due to accelerated globalisation. This has helped in China making huge economic growth, it is unlikely that China will try to subvert the system which has contributed much to its rise. The issue may be trying to shepherd the international trading system to its own advantage. This is one of the US worries over East Asia closed regionalism. But the countries are interdependent and those who are big exporters and have amassed huge current account surplus, also help those countries which are importing by providing them cheap goods, raw material and intermediary goods and labour. Chinese economic growth, it is difficult to foresee the countries which are used to comfortable lifestyle from cheap Chinese exports will like to forego it. But the problem remains that of managing or shepherding the present system in one's favour, like the way China is accused of keeping Yuan too cheap.

Though convergences on trade is an important determinant of present international relations. This has become the new orthodoxy of bilateral and multilateral relations. But one cannot be ignorant that this is leading to a new class of haves and have-nots. Both within domestic societies and globally. How states resolve this dilemma of maintaining trade relations and reducing trade imbalances is important? Will this fact lead to long term reordering of international relations is difficult to say? In one way this could catapult into greater regionalisation of international economic relations. Increasing regionalisation has a basis in the good economics as well, where overhead costs like transportation are reduced. But in the long term one can say that despite teething troubles of many trading arrangements, states will find ways to overcome or bypass the obstacles relating to trade.

It may be correct that in the present international system states have turned into trading states. That is, states are trading states, those which are not they try their best to be a trading state. But this fact of being trading state does not diminish the fact that states still have monopoly over legitimate physical coercion. If one has instruments of power, one may very well use it. That is, capabilities versus intentions debate ensue. Military power is most likely to act as a deterrent. But at the same time states with bigger military power are likely to bring their superior weight into play. It is in the latter context that China's rise raises apprehension. East Asian states have witnessed a number of incidents 1995 Mischief Reef incident, Impeccable Crisis, Spratly's issue, and Taiwan, Cheonan incident. Therefore, potential of armed conflict and coercion always exist.

Though, at the same time it may be said that costs will outbid benefit of any armed conflict. But Asia-Pacific is likely to witness an intensified competition. Despite the peace dividend, the region still sees high arms spending. It may be governed by historical animosities and factors, than the value of the events themselves. It is the North East Asia, which is under a long spell of peace, may once again see the action. North East Asia is still strategically poised, for which to maintain equilibrium will require active diplomacy from the stakeholders. Though, active diplomacy may in the short term worsen the situation. Make things unmanageable, for the very fact that picture has not emerged clearer. China's position is anticipatory, US presence helps to dampen this anxiety. Japan, inordinately relies on its special relationship with the United States. China is the most important variable, which brings uncertainty to the regional situation. As happens with the power transition, reordering of relationships takes place. This re-ordering may be accompanied by unsettling existent relationship. To dampen this anxiety, an appropriate international institution may be helpful. Big states can afford to not having it and small states can't generate it. In this vacuum ASEAN plays an important role, affording states a platform to engage. But this once again becomes hostage to a number of factors, in which the most important determinant will be the respective positions of the state and the interdependency they develop.

One of the problems of international relations has been how to account for change, rather preventing too much change occurring too soon. Perhaps it is why strategic studies are a conservative discipline, focussing on order. It will be difficult to foresee the exact situation emerging in a decade or two. But some scenarios can be foreseen, and long term trends needs to be emphasised. The most important is that, Asia will be new the focus of action. Though, this assertion has become a cliché, but it import is yet to be fully realised. First, is the most important aspect of Asianising Asia, that is, *autonomising* their relations, with lesser importance to Western powers. This may appeal to the nationalist sentiment of Asians, but some facts need to be emphasised. First, the presence of US looms larger in the strategic relations of Asia, which is likely to continue for a long time. Asia's salience is increasing, as evident from many developments. But Asianising Asia is welcome, in the form of economic importance and strategic autonomy, but the moot point is whether this will percolate within. Asian countries have characteristically emphasised social over individual, this has led to many exclusionary practices within societies. China's domestic troubles, and continues its policy of suppression in Tibet, Xinjiang, political dissidents as emerged in Tiananmen incident of 1989. It is difficult to say that language of rights, liberty and democracy has become part of Rise of Asia discourse. Worsts case of human rights abuses in many countries can be attributed at the states door. In their reactionary approach the Asian countries still ascribe these discourses as Western. It is no coincidental that states which appear strong internationally appear to be fraying within, this is true for most of the Asia-Pacific countries. China, India, Indonesia, Pakistan, Myanmar and Thailand are some of the prominent examples. It may point to the intractability of establishment of domestic order, but also it may have international ramifications. In these countries many of the problems are Janus faced, with external linkages, Tibet- India, Kashmir-Pakistan, and Taiwan-US.

Thus, in Asia-Pacific security dilemma has a domestic element, which is likely to feed on each other. In 2007, annual ASEAN Summit was not able to held because of disturbances in Hua Hin, Thailand.

In these complexities it is difficult to glean Chinese Asia-Pacific strategy, as policy announcements are few, and they are couched in larger ideological terminology, like world peace, multi-polarity and anti-hegemonism. However, gradually Chinese have begun to take an active interest in the international affairs with goal of shaping or influencing things rather than sitting on side-lines. It is axiomatic that Chinese foreign and security policy has been shaped by its domestic determinants in terms of strategic culture, national history and geographic location. But this applies more in case of China than other. It is this cultural specificity that fuels China Study in the contemporary world.

Historically, China has suffered from the vagaries of colonialism, remembered as a "century of shame and humiliation". This has generated a victim mentality in the China. But this victim mentality also fuels a deep set of xenophobic attitudes, which explains why China was unwilling to enter into multilateral mechanism surrounding its periphery. It saw them as western means out to harm Chinese interests. This suspicion was difficult to remove from their consciousness, which they were successful in dealing with, through the mechanism of "crossing the river by feeling stones". Yet, it affects their national outlook, in which they are still hesitant of many institutional mechanisms. This has to do with their strategic culture and outlook, which is affected by its history. Geopolitically, China has at the same time an entitlement mentality and compensatory approach.

The Chinese strategic culture has a dual or dialectical element, as asserted by authors like Johnston,[1] Scobell[2]. Their strategic culture has the twin strands of offensive as well as defensive. The former is termed by Johnston as *parabellum* strategic culture. In this twin strands former is dominant. It has also to do with their self-image of victim which propels them to be offensive and as well as reasonable and passive. Thus, in their strategic culture they combine with mutual contradictory tendencies like "active defense", which can be a perfect foil for pre-emptive war. Thus for them many historical wars were of necessity, foisted by the enemy. Even1962 war with India was a defensive war. This has also to do with the militant struggle of communism, where leaders have not only to guide people's movement but also interpret them. Thus for them everything becomes a tactical issue, Goldstein terms "present Chinese strategy comes with an expiry date."[3] Even the policy of peaceful rise or development is tactical strategy which helps in removing suspicion about Chinese future strategic behaviour.[4] The corollary of the fact that every thing even high principles are tactical, is that every thing is linked in Chinese strategic outlook. That is they have multidimensional view or spectral analysis of things. Therefore, it is difficult to arrive at closure. It especially makes Chinese future strategic behaviour an open ended question.

It is in this background that Chinese Asia-Pacific strategy was discussed. China has an entitlement mentality, which wants to reclaim its status especially in Asia-Pacific. There are still doubts over China's ambitions at the global stage. If Chinese are very much guided by their historical pattern of relationship and world view, they will likely restrict themselves to East Asia or Asia-Pacific. In East Asia they will like to enact Chinese middle kingdom complex. In this they will be guided by what can be called a policy of *concessionary balancing*. This policy atypical of Chinese dual policy involves both concessions and balancing. Both small and big powers give concessions or grant to each other, but will be done in the overall background of military balance. That is Chinese will like to see an

East Asia hierarchical order built around its overall military superiority. China could be said to earnestly following this strategy. Many states response in dual policies rather than hindering Chinese geopolitical goals is likely to advance its aims.

China has used multilateral fora provided by ASEAN to counter its suspicion in the neighbourhood. The neighbourhood instead of talking about balancing is talking about hedging, and simultaneously recognises that many instrument of hedging like Japan-US alliance, will in future fail to meet its objectives. ASEAN with grouping of ten nations of varied sizes, are doing best what smaller nations do best at, that is, propagating norms. It is not difficult to guess that once China has risen. The situation will much depend upon the attitudes of bigger powers like US, Russia, India and Japan. At present these powers are hedging their future bets and want to take part in regions economic growth story. Though overtly need is felt for an apposite multilateral body which can be commensurate with China's future growth, any top down approach is not taking place. Also, any bottom-up approach like Australian proposal of Asia Pacific Community is unlikely to be successful.

India's options are limited in this context as it will not fall into Chinese traditional hierarchical East Asian order. It is not meant that it would have been any better, but that benefits of *concessions* will be slight. Rather, whatever will be it will be through intense economic competition. India is more likely to fall under the balancing side of Chinese foreign security policy, this is very well evident in recent developments in the relations. Like developments around Sino-Indian border, border violations and China's plans to set up military bases in Pakistan. Policy options for India are limited, the most important is that India will have to increase its systemic power potential through all means, that is economic, diplomatic and military. Further, if India wants its neighbourhood to be peaceful it has to expand its geopolitical footprint to the Eastern most side of Asia. This will not only act as a pressure on China but also to prevent particularising tendency of China led East Asia and make it follow universal rules of international diplomatic and economic engagement. As, the power increases states like to create a sphere of influence, in which they try to exclude other powers. This has been the over-riding apprehension of US, India, Japan and Southeast Asian countries. Therefore, proper response becomes imperative.

Endnotes

[1] Alastair Iain Johnston, *Cultural Realism: Strategic Culture and Grand Strategy in Chinese History* (Princeton: Princeton University Press, 1995),

[2] Andrew Scobell, *China and Strategic Culture* (Carlisle, PA: SSI, 2002).

[3] Avery Goldstein, *Rising to the Challenge: China's Grand Strategy and International Security* (Stanford: Stanford University Press, 2005).

[4] Lynch cites an incident, when a senior Chinese Communist Party Advisor Zheng Bijina, in a T elevision interview ac cepts the tactical v alue of "peacef ul rise" as having "discourse power ". Daniel L ynch, " Chinese Thinking on the Futur e of International Relations: Realism as the *Ti,* Rationalism as the *Yong* ?, *The China Quarterly* ,197, Mar ch 2009, p .88.

Select Bibliography

Primary Documents

China's National Defense in 2008, Information Office of the State Council of the People's Republic of China January 2009, Beijing, available in pdf format at http://www.fas.org/programs/ssp/nukes/2008DefenseWhitePaper_Jan2009.pdf.

Government of Japan, Ministry of Foreign Affairs, "Joint Statement of the U.S.-Japan Security Consultative Committee Marking the 50th Anniversary of the Signing of The U.S.-Japan Treaty of Mutual Cooperation and Security", January 19, 2010, available at http://www.mofa.go.jp/region/n-america/us/security/joint1001.html.

Hill, Christopher R. Assistant Secretary for East Asian and Pacific Affairs, "Emergence of China in the Asia-Pacific: Economic and Security Consequences for the U.S." in testimony before the Senate Foreign Relations Committee, Subcommittee on East Asian and Pacific Affairs available at http://www.state.gov/p/eap/rls/rm/2005/47334.htm

Government of Australia, Ministry of Defence, *Defending Australia in the Asia Pacific Century: Force 2030,* Defence White Paper 2009 available at http://www.defence.gov.au/whitepaper/docs/defence_white_paper_2009.pdf.

The 2008 Pew Global Attitudes Survey in China: The Chinese Celebrate Their Roaring Economy, As they Struggle with Its Costs near Universal Optimism about Beijing Olympics. July 22, 2008, available at http://pewglobal.org/2008/07/22/the-chinese-celebrate-their-roaring-economy-as-they-struggle-with-its-costs/.

Government of India, Ministry of External Affairs, *Annual Report 2009-2010*, Policy Planning and Research Division, New Delhi, available at http://meaindia.nic.in/

Pranab Mukherjee's address " India's Look East Policy" at the Institute of Foreign Affairs and National Security, Republic of Korea, on 17th October 2007, available at, http://meaindia.nic.in/index.htm.

Central Intelligence Agency, *The World Factbook,* available at https://www.cia.gov/library/publications/the-world-factbook/rankorder/2147rank.html?countryName=Indonesia&countryCode=id®ionCode=eas&rank=16#id.

Remarks by H.E. Dr Surin Pitsuwan, Secretray General of ASEAN on the occasion of visit by HE Dai Bingguo, State Councilor of People's Republic of China at ASEAN Secretariat on 22 January 2010, available at http://www.aseansec.org/24206.htm.

" ASEAN- China Dialogue Relations" available at http://www.aseansec.org/5874.htm.

"ASEAN-China Investment Agreement" available at http://www.aseansec.org/Fact%20Sheet/AEC/2009-AEC-031.pdf.

" ASEAN trade by selected partner Country?Region, Table 19" available at http://www.aseansec.org/Stat/Table19.pdf.

"Top ten country/regional sources of visitors to ASEAN" available at http://www.aseansec.org/Stat/Table30.pdf.

Remarks by Premier Wen Jiabao At the First China-Japan-ROK Business Summit Remarks by Premier Wen Jiabao At the First China-Japan-ROK Business Summit available at http://www.fmprc.gov.cn/eng/wjdt/zyjh/t623025.htm.

"Embrace New Opportunities for China- ASEAN Cooperation" Address by HE Dai Bingguo, State Councillor of the Peoples Republic of China at ASEAN Secretariat on 22 January 2010, available at http://www.fmprc.gov.cn/eng/zxxx/t653431.htm.

"China's Position Paper on the New Security Concept"ÿJuly 31, 2002 ÿ http://www.mfa.gov.cn/eng/wjb/zzjg/gjs/gjzzyhy/2612/2614/t15319.htm.

"Joint Statement on the Tenth Anniversary of Trilateral Cooperation among the People's Republic of China, Japan and the Republic of Korea", Beijing China, 10 October 2009" available at http://www.mofa.go.jp/region/asia-paci/jck/meet0910/joint-1.pdf.

SIPRI Yearbook 2009: Armaments, Disarmament and International Security (Oxford: OUP, 2009).

Secondary Sources

Books

Ba, Alice D., *Re[Negotiating] East and South East Asia: Region, Regionalism and ASEAN* (Stanford University Press, 2009).

Barry, Theodore de Twing Tsit Chan and Burton Watson, *Introduction to Oriental Civilizations: Sources of Chinese Tradition* (New York, Columbia University Press, 1960).

Bergstern, C Fred, *Toward a Free Trade Area of the Asia-Pacific,* Policy Brief PB07-2, February 2007, Peterson Institute of International Economics, available at http://www.iie.com/publications/pb/pb07-2.pdf.

Bergstern, C. Fred, *China and Economic Integration in East Asia: Implications for the United States,* Policy Briefs in International Economics, Number PB07-3 available at http://www.iie.com/publications/pb/pb07-3.pdf.

Bert, Wayne, *The United States, China and Southeast Asian Security: A Changing of the Guard?* (Hampshire: Macmillan, 2003).

Bisley, Nick, *Building Asia's Security,* Adelphi Paper, 408, (London; Routledge, 2010).

Bull, Hedley, *Anarchical Society: Study of Order in World Politics* (New York, Sussex: Columbia University Press, 1995).

Burles, Mark and Abram N. Shulsky, *Patterns in China's Use of Force: Evidence from History and Doctrinal Writings* (Santa Monica, CA: Rand, 2000).

Buzan, Barry and Ole Weaver, *Regions and Powers: The Structure of International Security* (Cambridge: Cambridge University Press, 2003).

Calder, Kent E. "*Japan's* Energy Angst and Caspian Great Game", *NBR Analysis,* Vol 12, No,1, March 2001.

Campbell, Kurt and Derek J Mitchell, "Crisis in the Taiwan Strait?" in Siddharth Mohandas ed., *The Rise of China* (New York: Council on Foreign Relations Book 2002).

Chan, John, "Australia Call for "Asia-Pacific Community": A Sign of Growing Tensions" *World Socialist Website,* www.wsws.org. 27 June 2008.

Chan, Steve, *China, The US, and the Power-Transition Theory: A Critique* (Routledge: London and New York, 2008).

Chanlett- Avery, Emma and Vaughn, Bruce, "Emerging Trends in the Security Architecture in Asia: Bilateral and Multilateral Ties Among the United States, Japan, Australia and India", *CRS Report for Congress, January 7, 2008.*

Clinton, Hillary, " Remarks on Regional Architecture in Asia: Principles and Priorities" available at http://www.state.gov/secretary/rm/2010/01/135090.htm.

Copeland, Dale, "Economic Interdependence and the Future of US-Chinese Relations" in G John Ikenberry and Michael Mastanduno, ed, *International Relations Theory and the Asia-Pacific* (New York: Columbia University Press, 2003).

Dellios, Rosita, *Modern Chinese Defence Strategy: Present Development, Future Directions* (Hampshire; Macmillan, 1989).

Devare, Sudhir, *India and Southeast Asia: Towards Security Convergence* (New Delhi, ISEAS, Capital, 2006).

Dutt, Gargi and VP Dutt, *China after Mao* (New Delhi, Vikash, 1991).

Economy, Elizabeth and Michel Oskenberg, eds., *China Joins the World: Progress and Prospects* (New York, CFR, 1999).

Economy, Elizabeth, *The River Runs Black: The Environmental Challenges to China's Future* (New York: Cornell University Press, 2004).

Fairbank, John K., Edwin O. Resichauer and Albert M. Craig, *East Asia: Tradition and Transformation* (London: George Allen & Unwin Ltd., 1973).

Fairbank, John King, *China: A New History* (Cambridge, Massachusetts, London: The Belknap Press, 1992).

Feng, Huiyun, *Chinese Strategic Culture and Foreign Policy Decision Making: Confucianism, Leadership and War* (Routledge: London and New York, 2007).

Goh, Evelyn, *Meeting the China Challenge: The US in Southeast Asian Regional Security Strategies,* (Washington: East-West Center, 2005).

Goldstein, Avery, *Rising to the Challenge: China's Grand Strategy and International Security* (Stanford: Stanford University Press, 2005).

Gray, Colin S, *Modern Strategy* (Oxford, Oxford University Press, 1999).

Gungwu, Wang, "China and Southeast Asia: The Context of a New Beginning" in David Shambaugh, ed., *Power Shift: China and Asia's New Dynamics* (Berkeley: University of California Press, 2005).

Gungwu, Wang "Early Ming Relations with Southeast Asia: A Background Essay", John K. Fairbank ed., *The Chinese World Order: Traditional China's Foreign Relations* (HUP, Oxford 1968).

Gupta, Ranjit, "India's 'Look East' Policy", in Atish Sinha and Madhup Mohta, eds., *Indian Foreign Policy Challenges and Opportunities* (New Delhi: Academic Foundation, 2007).

Hong, Cai Peng, 'Non-traditional Security and China and ASEAN Relations: Co-operation, Commitments and Challenges,' in Ho Khai Leong and Samuel C. Y. Ku, (eds.), *China and Southeast Asia: Global Challenges and Regional Challenges* (Singapore: ISEAS, 2005).

Hook, Brian and Denis Twitchett eds., *The Cambridge Encyclopedia of China* (Cambridge, Cambridge University Press, 1991) 2nd Edition.

Hung, Jae Ho, "China's Ascendancy and the Korean Peninsula: From Interest Re-evaluation to Strategic Realignment? in David Shambaugh, ed., *Power Shift: China and Asia's New Dynamics* (Berkeley: University of California Press 2005).

Iida, Masafumi, "Japan-China Relations in East Asia: Rivals or Partners", Masafumi Iida, eds., *China's Shift: Global Strategy of the Rising Power* (Tokyo: NIDS, 2009).

Ji, You, *The Armed Forces of China* (London, New York: I.B. Tauris, 1999).

Johnston, Alastair Iain, *Cultural Realism: Strategic Culture and Grand Strategy in Chinese History* (Princeton: Princeton University Press, 1995).

Jun, Tsunekawa, "Toward a Stable Relationship between Japan and China: From a Bilateral to Multilateral Approach", Masafumi Iida ed., *China's Shift: Global Strategy of the Rising Power* (Tokyo, NIDS, 2009).

Kang, David C, *China Rising: Peace, Power, and Order in East Asia* (Sussex, Columbia University Press, 2007).

Katzenstein, Peter J., *A World of Regions: Asia and Europe in the American Imperium* (Ithaca, NY: Cornell University Press, 2005).

Kennedy, Paul, *The Rise and Fall of Great Powers: Economic Exchange and Military Conflict from 1500 to 2000* (New York: Random House, 1987).

Keohane, Robert O, *After Hegemony: Cooperation and Discord in World Political Economy* (Princeton: Princeton University Press, 1984).

Kim, Samuel S, "Northeast Asia in the Local-Regional-Global Nexus: Multiple Challenges and Contending Explanations", Samuel S. Kim, *International Relations of Northeast Asia.* (Lanham, Rowman & Littlefield Publishers, 2004).

Kim, Samuel S., "China and the United Nations", in Elizabeth Economy and Michel Oskenberg, eds., *China Joins the World: Progress and Prospects* (New York, CFR, 1999).

Kumar, Nagesh, "India and broader economic integration in Asia", in Atish Sinha and Madhup Mohta, eds., *Indian Foreign Policy Challenges and Opportunities* (New Delhi: Academic Foundation, 2007).

Lapid, Yosef and Friedrich Kratochwil, eds., *The Return of Culture and Identity in IR Theory* (Boulder, Colo.: Lynne Rienner, 1996).

Li, Nan, "The PLA's Evolving War fighting Doctrine, Strategy and Tactics, 1985-1995: A Chinese Perspective", David Shambaugh and Richard H. Yang, ed., *China's Military in Transition* (Oxford: Clarendon Press, 1997).

Macmillan, Alan Ken Booth and Russell Trood, "Strategic Culture", in Alan Macmillan, Ken Booth and Russell Trood, *Strategic Cultures in the Asia-Pacific Region* (New York, St. Martin's Press, 1999).

Sandhu, PJS, ed., *Rising China: Opportunity or Strategic Challenge* (New Delhi: Vij Books Pvt. Ltd, 2010).

Medeiros, Evan S. and others, *Pacific Currents: The Responses of US Allies and Security Partners in East Asia to China's Rise* (Santa Monica, Rand, 2008).

Medeiros, Evan S., *China's International Behaviour: Activism, Opportunism, and Diversification* (Santa Monica, CA, Rand, 2009).

Michael Oskenberg and Elizabeth Economy, "Introduction: China Joins the World" in Elizabeth Economy and Michael Oksenberg, eds., *China Joins the World: Progress and Prospects* (New York: Council on Foreign Relations, 1999).

Migdal, Joel S., Atul Kohli and Vivienne Shue, eds., *State Power and Social Forces: Domination and Transformation in the Third World* (Cambridge: Cambridge University Press, 1994).

Nehru, Jawaharlal, *Discovery of India* (New Delhi: Jawaharlal Nehru Memorial Fund/ Oxford University Press, 1946, (1998)).

Nye, Joseph S, *Soft Power: The Means to Success in World Politics* (Harvard: Public Affairs, 2004).

Parker, Geoffery, *The Military Revolution: Military Innovation and the Rise of the West, 1500-1800*(Cambridge: Cambridge University Press, 1996).

Pillsbury, Michael, *China; Debates the Future Security Environment* (Washington DC: NDU, 2000).

Pollpeter, Kevin, "The Chinese Vision of Space Military Operations", James Mulvenon and David Finkelstein, eds., *China's Revolution in Doctrinal Affairs: Emerging Trends in the Operational Art of the Chinese People's Liberation Army* (Alexandria, Virginia: The CNA, 2005).

Quinlan, Joseph P, "Ties That Bind", in?" Siddharth Mohandas, *The Rise of China* (New York: CFR, 2002).

Rajasimman, S, "China-ASEAN Relations- Emerging Asian Security Architecture", in Srikanth Kondapalli and Emi Mifune, *China and Its Neighbours* (New Delhi: Pentagon Press, 2006).

Raman, B, *The Kaoboys of R&AW: Down Memory Lane* (New Delhi: Lancer, 2007).

Rao, P.V., (ed.), *India and ASEAN: Partners at Summit* (New Delhi: KW Publishers, 2008).

Ross, Robert S, "Engagement in US China Policy" in Alistair Ian Johnston and Robert S Ross, eds., *Engaging China: The Management of an Emergent Power* (London: Routledge, 1999).

Sanders, David, " International Relations: Neo-Realism and Neo-liberalism", in Robert E. Goodin and Hans- Dieter Klingeman eds., *A New Handbook of Political Science* (Oxford, Oxford University Press, 1996).

Segal, Gerald, "Does China Matter?" Siddharth Mohandas, *The Rise of China* (New York: CFR, 2002).

Segal, Gerald, *Defending China* (Oxford: Oxford University Press, 1985).

Shambaugh, David, "Return to the Middle Kingdom? China and Asia in the Early Twenty-First Century" David Shambaugh, ed., *Power Shift:*

China and Asia's New Dynamics (Berkeley: University of California Press, 2005).

Shirk, Susan L., *China: The Fragile Superpower* (New York: Oxford University Press, 2007).

Shue, Vivienne "State Power and Social Organisation in China", Joel S. Migdal, Atul Kohli and Vivienne Shue, eds. *State Power and Social Forces: Domination and Transformation in the Third World* (Cambridge: Cambridge University Press, 1994).

Sikri, Rajiv, *Challenge and Strategy: Rethinking India's Foreign Policy* (New Delhi, Sage, 2009).

Solomon, Richard H, *Chinese Negotiating Behaviour: Pursuing Interests Through 'Old Friends'* (Washington: USIP, 1999).

Swaine, Michael D. and Ashley J. Tellis, *Interpreting China's Grand Strategy: Past, Present, and Future* (Rand, Santa Monica, 2000).

Thuy, Do Thi, *The Implementation of Vietnam- China Land Border Treaty: Bilateral and Regional Implications* (Singapore; S Rajaratnam School of International Studies, 2009), Working Paper 173, 5 March 2009 available at http://www3.ntu.edu.sg/rsis/publications/WorkingPapers/WP173.pdf.

Tow, William T. eds., *Security in the Asia-Pacific: A Regional- Global Nexus?* (Cambridge; Cambridge University Press, 2009).

Waltz, Kenneth N., *Theory of International Politics* (Reading: Addison Wesley, 1979).

Yuan, Jing Dong, *China-ASEAN Relations: Perspectives, Prospects and Implication for U.S. Interests* (Carlisle P.A., Strategic Studies Institute, 2006).

Zhang, Tiejun, "East Asian Community and China", in Jiemian Yang et al, *Asian Regionalism on the Rise and International System in Transformation* (Shanghai: SIIS, 2007).

Zhang, Yunling and Tang Shiping, "China's National Strategy", in David Shambaugh eds., *Power Shift: China and Asia's New Dynamic* (Los Angeles: University of California Press, 2005).

Journals

Ba, Alice, "Systemic Neglect? A Reconsideration of US-Southeast Asia Policy", *Contemporary South East Asia,* Vol. 31, No. 3, 2009.

Bitzinger, Richard A., *"A New Arms Race? Explaining Recent Southeast Asian Military Acquisitions", Contemporary Southeast Asia*, Vol 32, No. 1, 2010.

Buszynski, Leszek, "Russia and Southeast Asia: A New Relationship", *Contemporary Southeast Asia,* Vol 28, No. 2, 2006.

Buszynski, Leszek, "Sino-Japanese Relations: Interdependence, Rivalry and Regional Security", *Contemporary Southeast Asia,* Vol 31, no. 1, 2009.

Cai, Yongshun, "Local Governments and the Suppression of Popular Resistance in China", *The China Quarterly,* no. 193, 2008.

Castro, Renato Cruz De, " The US- Phillipine Alliance: An Emerging Hedge Against an Emerging China Challenge", *Contemporary Southeast Asia,* Vol 31, No. 3, 2009.

Chen, Jie and Bruce J. Dickson, "Allies of the State: Democratic Support and Regime Support among China's Private Entrepreneurs", *The China Quarterly,* no. 196, 2008.

Chey, Hyoung-kyu "The Changing Political Dynamics of East Asian Financial Cooperation: The Chiang Mai Initiative, *Asian Survey,* Vol. 49, Issue 3, 2009.

Chneg-Chwee, Kuik, "The Essence of Hedging: Malaysia and Singapore's Response to a Rising China", *Contemporary South East Asia,* Vol. 30, No.2, 2008.

Christoffersen, Gaye, "Russia's breakthrough into the Asia-Pacific: China's role", *International Relations Of the Asia-Pacific,* Vol 10, No.1. 2010.

Chung, Ching-peng, " The "Good Neighbour Policy" in the Context of China's Foreign Relations", *China: An International Journal*, Vol 7 , No. 1, Mar.2009.

Shambaugh, David, "China Engages Asia: Reshaping the Regional Order", *International Security,* Vol. 29, No.3, (Winter 2004/2005).

Dosch, Jorn, "Vietnam's ASEAN Membership Revisited; Golden Opportunity or Golden Cage", *Contemporary Southeast Asia,* Vol 28, No. 2, 2006.

Drezner, Daniel W, "Bad Debts; Assessing China's Financial Influence in Great Power Politics", *International Security*, Vol. 34, No. 1, Fall 2009.

Dutta, Sujit, "Securing the Sea Frontier: China's Pursuit of Sovereignty Claims in the *South* China Sea", *Strategic Analysis,* Vol. 29, No. 2, Apr-Jun 2005.

Egretau, Reneaud, "India's Ambitions in Burma: More Frustration Than Success?" *Asian Survey*, 48, 6, 2008.

Emmers, Ralf, "Regional Hegemonies and The Exercise of Power in Southeast Asia: A Study of Indonesia and Japan", *Asian Survey,* Vol. 45, Issue 4, July/ August 2005.

Emmerson, Donald K., "Challenging ASEAN: A "Topological" View", *Contemporary Southeast Asia,* Vol 29, No.3, 2007.

Feffer, John, "An Arms Race in Northeast Asia?" *Asian Perspective,* Vol.33, No. 4, 2009.

Feng, Zhu "An Emerging Trend in East Asia: Military Budget Increases and their Impact", *Asian Perspective,* Vol. 33, No. 4, 2009.

Garver, John W., "Development of China's Overland Transportation Links with Central, South-West and South Asia", *The China Quarterly,* 185, 2006.

Ghosh, Madhuchanda, "India and Japan's Growing Synergy: From a Political to a Strategic Focus", *Asian Survey,* 48, 2, 2008.

Goldtsein, Avery, "The Diplomatic Face of China's Grand Strategy: A Rising Power's Emerging Choice", *The China Quarterly*, Vol. 168, 2001.

Gray, Colin S, "In Praise of International Studies", *Review of International Studies,* Vol 29, 2003

Hays Gries, "China's "New Thinking" on Japan", *The China Quarterly,* Vol.184, 2005

Hong, Zhao. "India and China: Rivals or Partners in Southeast Asia", *Contemporary Southeast Asia,* Vol. 29, No. 1, 2007.

Hwee, Yeo Lay, "Japan, ASEAN, and the Construction of an East Asian Community", *Contemporary Southeast Asia,* Vol. 28, No. 2, 2006.

Ikenberry, G John, "The Rise of China and the Future of West: Can the Liberal System Survive", *Foreign Affairs,* January/February 2008.

Johnston, Alastair Iain "Is China a Status Quo Power?", *International Security,* Vol 27, No.4 (Spring 2003).

Kang, David C., "Getting Asia Wrong: The Need for New Analytical Frameworks", *International Security,* Vol 27, No. 4, Spring 2003.

Katsumata, Hiro, " Reconstruction of Diplomatic Norms in Southeast Asia: The Case for Strict Adherence to the "ASEAN Way", *Contemporary Southeast Asia,* Volume 25, Number 1, April 2003.

Keat, Tok Sow, "Neither Friends Nor Foes; China's Dilemmas in Managing in its Japan Policy", *China: An International Journal* 3, 2 (Sep 2005).

Kleine- Ahlbrandt, Stephanie and Andrew Sall, "China's New Dictatorship Diplomacy: Is Beijing Parting with Pariahs", *Foreign Affairs,* January/ February 2008.

Kurlantzick, Joshua, "China's Charm Offensive in Southeast Asia," in *Current History,* September 2006.

Lam, Willy, "China's Political Feet of Clay", *Far Eastern Economic Review,* October 2009, Vol. 172, No.8.

Lampton, David M., "The United States and China in the Age of Obama: looking each other straight in the eyes." *Journal of Contemporary China,* 18(62), 2009.

Layne, Christopher "Offshore Balancing Revisited", *The Washington Quarterly,* Vol. 25, No. 2, Spring 2002.

Layne, Christopher "The Unipolar Illusion: Why New Great Power Will Rise," *International Security,* Vol.17, No.4 (Spring 1993).

Layne, Christopher "The Unipolar Illusion Revisited: The Coming End of the United States' Unipolar Moment", *International Security,* Vol.31, No.2, (Fall 2006).

Layne, Christopher, "China's Challenge to US Hegemony," *Current History,* January 2008.

Li, Lianjiang and Kevin J. O'Brien, "Protest Leadership in China", *The China Quarterly,* No. 193, March 2008.

Limaye, Satu P., "United States- ASEAN Relations on ASEAN's Fortieth Anniversary: A Glass Half Full", *Contemporary Southeast Asia,* Vol 29, No.3, 2007.

Lin, Chong-pin "Beijing's New Grand Strategy: An Offensive with Extra- Military Instruments" available at http://www.asianresearch.org/articles/2983.html.

Luong, Dinh Thi Hien, " Vietnam- Japan Relations in the Context of Building an East Asian Community", *Asia- Pacific Review,* Vol. 16, No. 1, 2009.

Lynch, Daniel " Chinese Thinking on the Future of International Relations: Realism as the *Ti,* Rationailsm as the *Yong*? *The China Quarterly,* 197, March 2009,

Manicom, James, "Sino-Japanese Cooperation in the East China Sea: Limitations and Prospects", *Contemporary Southeast Asia,* Vol. 30. No. 3, 2008.

Mohan, C Raja, "India and the Balance of Power", *Foreign Affairs,* July/ August 2006.

Murphy, Ann Marie, "Beyond Balancing and Bandwagoning: Thailand's Response to China's Rise", *Asian Security,* Vol 6, No.1, 2007.

Naidu, G.V.C., 'Whither the Look East Policy: India and Southeast Asia', *Strategic Analysis*, Vol.28, No.2, Apr-Jun 2004.

Nair, Deepak, "Regionalism in the Asia-Pacific/ East Asia: A Frustrated Regionalism? *Contemporary Southeast Asia,* Vol 31, No. 1, 2008.

Nambiar, Satish, "A Role for India in the Emerging World Order", *USI Journal*, Vol CXXXVI, No. 563, July-September 2006.

Odgaard, Liselotte, "Chinese Northeast Asia policies and the tragedy of Northeast Asia's Security Architecture", *Global Change, Peace & Security,* Vol.20, No.2, June 2008.

Pomfret, John and Blaine Harder, "Wary Japan redefines relationship with US", *The Washington Post,* 22 October 2009.

Qiang, Shen, "Pluralistic Geopolitics in East Asia: Evolving in Ups and Downs", *International Strategic Studies,* 4th June 2007.

Rathus, Joel, " Squaring the Japanese and Australia Proposals for an East Asian and Asia Pacific Community: is America in or out", November 4, 2009, available at http://www.eastasiaforum.org/2009/11/04/squaring-the-japanese-and-australia-proposals-for-an-east-asian-and-asia-pacific-community-is-america-in-or-out/ accessed on 18th November 2009.

Ross, Robert S. "The Geography of the Peace: East Asia in the Twenty First Century", *International Security*, 23, 4, 1999.

Ross, Robert S., "China's Naval Nationalism: Sources, Prospects and the US Responses", *International Security,* Vol. 34, No. 2, (Fall 2009).

Schmitt, Gary, "A Road Map for Asian-Pacific Security", *National Security Outlook*, available at http://www.aei.org/outlook/100926.

Scobell, Andrew, "Is there a civil-military gap in China's peaceful rise? "*Parameter* Vol. XXXIX, No.2, Summer 2009.

Scot- Tanner, Murray and Eric Green, " Principals and Secret Agents: Central versus Local Control Over Policing and Obstacles to "Rule of Law" in China", *The China Quarterly,* No.191, September, 2007.

Self, Benjamin, "China and Japan: A Façade of Friendship", *The Washington Quarterly*, 26, 1, Winter 2002-03.

Shambaugh, David, "China Engages Asia: Reshaping the Regional Order", *International Security,* Vol. 29, No.3, (Winter 2004/2005).

Shao,Yuqun, "The Shanghai Cooperation Organization and the Development of Sino-US Relations" in Jiemian Yang et al, *Asian Regionalism on the Rise and International System in Transformation* (Shanghai: SIIS, 2007).

Shekhar,Vibhanshu, *India- Singapore Relations: An Overview,* Special Report No. 41, June 2007.

Singh, Sinderpal and Syeda Sana Rahman, "India-Singapore Relations: Constructing a "New "Bilateral Relationship", *Contemporary Southeast Asia*, Vol 32, No. 1, 2010.

Singh, Swaran, "Mekong- Ganga Cooperation Initiative: Analysis and Assessment of India's Engagement with Greater Mekong Sub-region", IRASEC, Occasional Paper, No. 3, 2007.

Stuart –Fox, Martin "Southeast Asia and China: The role of History and Culture in Shaping Future Relations", *Contemporary Southeast Asia*, Vol. 26, No.1 2004, 128.

Sudo, Sueo, "Japan's ASEAN Policy: Reactive or Proactive in the face of a Rising China in East Asia", *Asian Perspective,* Vol. 33, No. 1, 2009.

Sukma, Rizal, "Indonesia-China Relations: The Politics of Engagement", *Asian Survey*, Vol 49, Issue 4, July/ August 2009.

Tanaka, Hitoshi, "A Japanese Perspective on China", *East Asia Insights: Toward Community Building,* Vol. 3, No. 2, 2008.

Tanaka, Hitoshi, "Defining Normalcy: The Future Course of Japan's Foreign Policy", *East Asia Insights: Toward Community Building,* Vol.3, No. 1, January 2008.

Thomas Lu et al, "China's "Soft Power" in Southeast Asia", *Congressional Research Service Report*, for Congress, January 4, 2008.

Vatikiotis, Michael R. J., "Catching the Dragons' tail: China and Southeast Asia in the 21st Century", *Contemporary Southeast Asia,* Vol. 25, Number 1, April 2003.

Vuving, Alexander L, "Strategy and Evolution of Vietnam's China Policy", *Asian Survey,* Vol, 36, No. 6, November/ December, 2006.

Wang, Yuan-Kang "China's Grand Strategy and US Primacy: Is China Balancing American Power" Brookings Institution, available at http:/ /www.brookings.edu/papers/2006/07china_wang.aspx

Wedeman, Andrew ´The Intensification of Corruption in China", *The China Quarterly,* No.180, December 2004.

White, Hugh, *A Focused Force: Australia's Defence Priorities in the New Century* (New South Wales, Lowy Institute, 2009).

Womack, Brantly, "China Between Region and World", *The China Journal,* No.61, January 2009.

Yang, Jian, "Of interest and distrust: Understanding China's Policy Towards Japan", *China: An International Journal,* 5, 2 (Sep.2007).

Yoshimatsu, Hidetaka, "The Rise of China and the Vision for an East Asian Community", *Journal of Contemporary China, 18* (62), November 2009.

Zaidi, S Akbar, 'South Asia? West Asia? Pakistan: Location, Identity', *Economic and Political Weekly,* March 7, 2009, Vol. XLIV No 10.

Zhang, Teijun, "Chinese Strategic Culture: Traditional and Present Features", *Comparative Strategy,* Vol.21,Issue 2, 2002.

Singha, Komol, "Indo-ASEAN Economic Integration", *South Asian Journal*, Vol. 25, September 2009.

Garver, John W., "The Restoration of Sino-Indian Comity Following India's Nuclear Tests", *The China Quarterly,* Vol. 168, 2001.

Goldstein, Avery, "The Diplomatic Face of China's Grand Strategy: A Rising Power's Emerging Choice", *The China Quarterly,* Vol 168, no. 1, 2001.

Wedeman, Andrew, "The Intensification of Corruption in China", *The China Quarterly,* No. 184, 2004.

Yoda, Tatsuro, " Japan's Host Nation Support Program for the US-Japan Security Alliance", *Asian Survey,* Vol. 46, No. 6, November/ December 2006.

Jones, David Martin and Michael L. R. Smith, "Making Process, Not Progress: ASEAN and the Evolving East Asian Regional Order", *International Security*, Vol 32, No. 1, (Summer 2007).

Scott, David, "Strategic Imperatives of India as an Emerging Player in Pacific Asia", *International Studies*, 44, 2, 2007.

Ling, LHM, Ching-Chane Hwang and Boyu Chen, " Subaltern straits: 'exit', 'voice', and 'loyalty' in the United States- China- Taiwan relations, *International Relations of the Asia-Pacific,* Vol. 10, 2010.

Ross, Robert S. and Aaron L. Friedberg, "Here Be Dragons", *The National Interest*, September/ October 2009.

Yahya, Faizal, "India and Southeast Asia: Revisited", *Contemporary Southeast Asia,* Vol 25, No. 1, April 2003.

Yu, Peter Kien-Hong, "The Chinese (Broken) U –shaped Line in the South China Sea: Points Lines, and Zones," *Contemporary Southeast Asia*, Vol.25, no. 3, 2003.

Beeson, Mark, "ASEAN Plus Three and the Rise of Reactionary Regionalism", *Contemporary Southeast Asia,* Vol 25, No. 2, August 2003.

Newspaper Articles

'China welcomes role of US in Asian-Pacific Area", *China Daily,* February17, 2009, available at http://www.chinadaily.com.cn/china/ 2009-02/17/content_7485786.htm.

'Crisis could be 'turning point' for Sino-US ties', *China Daily,* March 02, 2009, available at http://chinadaily.cn/china/2009-03/02/content_7525023.htm.

" 60 % of DPJ lower house members Japan want out of US nuclear Umbrella", *Japan Today,* 11th October, 2009, available at http://www.japantoday.com/category/politics/view/60-of-dpj-lower-house-members-want-japan-out-of-us-nuclear-umbrella.

"Government to postpone adoption of new defence outline to next year", *Japan Today*, 11 October 2009, available at http://www.japantoday.com/category/politics/view/govt-to-postpone-adoption-of-new-defense-outline-to-next-year.

"Indonesia told to initiate new Asia-Pacific Forum", *The Jakarta Post,* 6 May 2009 available at http://www.thejakartapost.com/news/2009/05/06/indonesia-told-initiate-new-asiapacific-forum.html.

Rao, Bhanoji "Does APEC Membership Really Matter for India" http://wwwthehindubusinesslinecom/2007/01/23/stories/2007012300050800'htm.

"Asia Free Trade Zone Raises Some Hopes, Some Fears About China", *International Herald Tribune,* January 1, 2010, available at http://www.nytimes.com/2010/01/01/business/global/01trade. html? scp= 1&sq=China-%20ASEAN% 20Free%20Trade% 20Area% 20&st=cse.

"China's Economic Power Unsettles the Neighbors", *The New York Times,* December 10, 2009, available at http://www.nytimes.com/2009/12/10/world/asia/10jakarta.html?_r=1.

"China's Significance to Malaysia is Growing", *People's Daily,* 23 June 2010 available at http://english.people.com.cn/90001/90776/90883/7036857.html, accessed on 5th July 2010.

Suryanarayna, P S, "Soft Focus on APEC geopolitics", *The Hindu,* November 2, 2009, available at, http://.thehindu.com/2009?11?02?stories, accessed on November 3, 2009.

"North Korea Talks For Peace Treaty Talks with US ", *International Herald Tribune,* 11 January 2010 , available at http://

www.nytimes.com/2010/01/12/world/asia/12korea.html? scp=1&sq=north%20%20korea%20steephen%20bos worth&st=cse.

"China Helps the Powerful in Namibia", *International Herald Tribune*, 20 November 2009, available at http://www.nytimes.com/2009/11/20/world/asia/20namibia.html? ref=asia&pagewanted=print.

"China's rise decades most read story" available at http://www.reuters.com/article/idUSTRE5B70AA20091208.

" China must address income gap first: World Bank Chief Economist", January 08, 2010, http://business.globaltimes.cn/comment/2010-01/497236.html.

Xiaohuo, Cui and Peng Kuang, "China-US defense talks best in decades", *China Daily,* March 02,2009, http://www.chinadaily.com.cn/china/2009-03/02/content_7524246.htm.

Tim Johnston, "Chinese Diaspora: Indonesia", http://news.bbc.co.uk/2/hi/asia-pacific/4312805.stm

www.ingramcontent.com/pod-product-compliance
Lightning Source LLC
Chambersburg PA
CBHW070810300326
41914CB00078B/1923/J

* 9 7 8 9 3 8 0 1 7 7 4 3 4 *